Happiness Is a Serious Problem

Happiness Is a Serious Problem

A Human Nature Repair Manual

Dennis Prager

ReganBooks

An Imprint of HarperCollins*Publishers*

HarperCollins books may be purchased for educational, business, or sales promotional use. For information please write: Special Markets Department, HarperCollins Publishers, Inc., 10 East 53rd Street, New York, NY 10022.

FIRST EDITION

Designed by Elliott Beard

Library of Congress Cataloging-in-Publication Data

Prager, Dennis, 1948–

    Happiness is a serious problem : a human nature repair manual / Dennis Prager. —1st ed.
      p. cm.
    ISBN 0-06-039219-3
    1. Happiness. I. Title.
    BF575.H27P73   1998
    158.1—dc21   97-35404

98 99 00 01 02 ❖/RRD 10 9 8 7 6 5 4 3 2

For Fran

Contents

CONTENTS

Part III
Attitudes and Behaviors That Are Essential to Happiness

Introduction

I never expected to write a book on happiness.

Despite a lifetime of writing and lecturing, until ten years ago I had written nothing and given almost no lectures on this subject. Like many other people, I had devoted a great deal of time to thinking through and struggling with the issue of happiness, but as far as lecturing, writing, and my radio talk show were concerned, I was preoccupied with other subjects—especially good and evil, theology, contemporary issues, and issues relating to male-female differences.

Why did I neglect happiness? Because I considered these other topics to be more serious and therefore more worthy of my time. I regarded happiness as essentially a light topic—even though I surely wanted to be happy and assumed that everyone else did too. My morality-comes-first attitude and religious background had led me to assume that concern with happiness was somehow a less than noble pursuit. People concerned with good and evil, I believed, should not devote much time to writing or speaking about being happy; and the relatively little that I had heard or read on the subject seemed to me either too rosy or too filled with clichés.

My attitude toward happiness was entirely wrong. Happiness is not a selfish or frivolous concern; it is as deep and worthy a subject as good and evil. Human beings want to be happy, and they have a right to want to be. Far from being a selfish or ignoble goal, this is one of the distinguishing features of human beings. To the extent that animals can be said to want anything, what they want is to avoid pain and to be sated, but not to be happy. For better and for worse, this is a uniquely human aim.

The story of how I came to learn this lesson about the significance of happiness and how I came to lecture more on this subject than on any other may interest the reader.

Ten years ago, I was invited by a clergyman at UCLA to deliver a lecture to students there. He told me that since my name was known to a number of students because of my Los Angeles radio talk show, he was assured of a turnout.

"I assume you want me to speak on religion," I said, since he was a clergyman and I frequently spoke on the subject.

"Oh, no," he responded. "No one will show up if you do. I would like you to speak on a light subject."

"Like what?" I asked.

"Like happiness."

"But happiness isn't a light subject," I protested. My first marriage had just broken up. "In fact, happiness is a serious problem," I told him.

"That's a great title," he responded.

And that is how it all began. He had given me the subject with which I would be preoccupied for ten years, the title of every talk I was to give on the subject, and the title of this book.

I worked hard on that speech. I was sure that it would be one of the few times I would ever lecture on the subject, and I wanted a tape of it. If it turned out to be a good speech, I would add it to the list of my tapes that I make available to the readers of my newsletter.

As it happened, I did like the way it turned out, and I added it to my tape list. Soon thereafter, it became my best-selling tape; a radio station in New York City broadcast it in its entirety; an editor at *Redbook* magazine heard the broadcast and asked me to write an article on happiness; *Reader's Digest* abridged the *Redbook* piece for publication in various languages; book offers came in, as did lecture invitations here and abroad. I have since given two full courses on happiness at a Jewish seminary, all-day courses on happiness to business groups around America, and have lectured on the subject on five continents.

None of this is intended to impress the reader. I relate it solely to explain why someone previously preoccupied with other issues would come to devote ten years to lecturing and ultimately writing a book on happiness. Although good and evil, theology, sex differences, and other issues remain great concerns of mine, once I began seeing how much these ideas about happiness helped contribute to the quality of people's lives, writing this book became almost a moral imperative.

My talks in various countries also had an impact on my writing this book. They confirmed what I could previously only suspect: that while cultures vary profoundly, the human desire for happiness is nearly universal, as are many of the obstacles to happiness.

Having explained why I have written this book, I feel obliged to offer some disclaimers.

First, I have not written this book in the belief that everyone who reads it will become happy. The very idea is preposterous. To be happy requires knowledge about how to achieve happiness (i.e., wisdom) and hard work and self-discipline to put that knowledge into practice. This book offers some of that knowledge and ideas about how to put it into practice. However, it cannot compel anyone to either incorporate the knowledge or put any of it into practice.

Second, I have not written this book in the belief that everyone can be equally happy. Some people will always be happier than others, just as some people will always play the piano better than others. But just as nearly all of us, with good teaching and self-discipline, could play the piano much better than we do now, nearly all of us, with good teaching and self-discipline, could be happier than we are now.

Third, I do not for a moment offer these ideas as the definitive or final words on happiness. There are many ways to lead a happy life; the ideas in this book are not the only roads that lead there.

Nevertheless, whatever road you choose, I would be surprised if *Happiness Is a Serious Problem* did not help you on that road.

Given the uniqueness of every individual, it is impossible to know how ideas on as personal an issue as happiness will be absorbed by all readers. I therefore showed various stages of this book to more people than anything else I have ever written, and I have learned from each of them.

I am particularly grateful to my capable and dedicated editor Todd Silverstein and to Joseph Telushkin, each of whom wrote incisive comments on virtually every page of the book. Their contributions, along with those of Allen Estrin, to whom I read aloud almost every page, were of immense importance to the final product. I am similarly grateful to Dr. Stephen Marmer, Zachary Schreier, and Laurie Zimmet, each of whom took time from their busy lives to read the manuscript and offer excellent suggestions.

My wife, Fran, has had to endure my preoccupation with happiness for some time. She has also graciously sat through many of my lectures on the subject, including four consecutive nights in four South American countries (in slower English, no less) and has read every word and made critical suggestions. She and our wonderful children, Anya, David, and Aaron, are already happier people—thanks to my finally finishing this book. As Fran has often put it, writing about happiness is a serious problem.

It will all be worth it if this book enables but one reader to better cope with the challenges of life and become a happier and better person. It is, of course, my great wish that many people will be so affected.

Part 1

Premises

Happiness Is a Serious Problem combines ideas about happiness with a practical guide to applying these ideas to your life. It is written in the form of a compendium of ideas and suggestions rather than as an extended essay. This reflects the systematic way in which I have thought through these ideas and presented them in lectures and on my radio talk show for the last ten years. This approach has the advantages of conciseness, clarity, and an ability to deal with every major aspect of happiness that I could identify. It has the disadvantage of not pursuing these many aspects in all their depth. To do that would have entailed writing a veritable encyclopedia of happiness.

The book is divided into three parts. Part I is a brief statement of the premises of the book. Part II describes what I believe are the greatest obstacles to happiness for most people—and thoughts on how to deal with those obstacles. Part III delineates what I believe are the major attitudes and behaviors necessary for achieving increased happiness.

While there is some methodology to the order of the chapters, the chapters of the book can be read in any order. Each chapter is largely a self-contained unit. However, although the order is not critical, reading all the chapters is.

Chapter 1

Happiness Is
a Moral Obligation

We tend to think that we owe it to ourselves to be as happy as we can be. And this is true. But happiness is far more than a personal concern. It is also a moral obligation.

After one of my talks on happiness, a woman in the audience stood up and said, "I only wish my husband had come to this talk." (He had chosen to attend a talk on business instead.) She explained that he was the unhappy one in their relationship and that much as she loved him, it was not easy being married to an unhappy person.

This woman enabled me to put into words what I had been searching for—the *altruistic,* in addition to the obvious *personal,* reasons to take happiness seriously. I told the woman and the audience that she was right; her husband should have attended the talk because *he had a moral obligation to his daily partner in life to be as happy as he could be.*

Upon a moment's reflection, this becomes obvious. We owe it to our husband or wife, our fellow workers, our children, our friends, indeed to everyone who comes into our lives, to be as happy as we can be. This does not mean acting unreal, and it certainly does not mean refraining from honest and intimate expressions of our feelings to

3

those closest to us. But it does mean that we owe it to others to work on our happiness. We do not enjoy being around others who are usually unhappy. Those who enter our lives feel the same way. Ask a child what it was like to grow up with an unhappy parent, or ask parents what pain they suffer if they have an unhappy child (of any age).

There is a second reason why happiness is a moral obligation. In general, people act more decently when they are happy. The chapter on seeking goodness explains the connection between goodness and happiness at length. It will suffice here to answer this: Do you feel more positively disposed toward other people and do you want to treat other people better when you are happy or when you are unhappy?

There is yet a third reason. I once asked a deeply religious man if he considered himself a truly pious person. He responded that while he aspired to be one, he felt that he fell short in two areas. One of those areas, he said, was his not being a happy enough person to be considered truly pious.

His point was that unhappy religious people reflect poorly on their religion and on their Creator. He was right; in fact, unhappy religious people pose a real challenge to faith. If their faith is so impressive, why aren't these devoted adherents happy? There are only two possible reasons: either they are not practicing their faith correctly, or they are practicing their faith correctly and the religion itself is not conducive to happiness. Most outsiders assume the latter reason. Unhappy religious people should therefore think about how important being happy is—if not for themselves, then for the sake of their religion. Unhappy, let alone angry, religious people provide more persuasive arguments for atheism and secularism than do all the arguments of atheists.

Chapter 2

Unhappiness Is Easy— Happiness Takes Work

I was raised never to take the easy way out. I didn't like this idea when I was a child, and my family sometimes carried it to an extreme, but this principle has served me very well as an adult.

The easy way *is* very often the wrong way.

In my late teens I started applying this attitude to unhappiness, and it has had a permanently positive effect on my life. I was not a particularly happy child, and I also had an early awareness of—and later preoccupation with—human evil and suffering. As a result, happiness did not come easily. Moreover, like most teenagers, I spent part of my teens reveling in my angst. One day, however, the thought occurred to me that being unhappy was easy—in fact, the easy way out—and that it took no courage, effort, or greatness to be unhappy. *Anyone* could be unhappy. True achievement, I realized at an early age, lay in struggling to be happy.

To this day, when I am unhappy I tell myself that I am taking the easy way out, that happiness is a battle to be waged and not a feeling to be awaited.

The notion that happiness must be constantly worked at comes as news—disconcerting news—to many people. They assume that happiness is a feeling and that this feeling comes as a result of good things that happen to them. We therefore have little control over how happy we are, the thinking goes, because we can control neither how we feel nor what happens to us.

This book is predicated on the opposite premise: Happiness is largely, though certainly not entirely, determined by *us*—through hard work (most particularly by controlling our nature) and through attaining wisdom (i.e., developing attitudes that enable us not to despair).

Everything worthwhile in life is attained through hard work. Happiness is not an exception.

Chapter 3

The Mind Plays
the Central Role

While most people think of happiness as almost entirely a heart-based feeling—"I feel happy, I feel unhappy"—the focus of this book is on the mind. The use of one's mind and intelligence is indispensable to achieving happiness. Why? Because in order to be happy, we constantly have to ask ourselves, "Will this—having this thing, taking this action, relating to this person, purchasing this item, even dwelling on this thought—make me happier or unhappier?" Answering these questions demands constant thought and reflection.

Most people do not regularly ask, "Will this make me happier?" before engaging in some action. Rather, they do what they do because it feels good at that moment.

That mind and intelligence are essential to happiness does not imply in any way that being a genius gives a person a better chance at being happy (on the contrary, geniuses are not known to be a particularly happy group of people). It does imply that people must use their minds to be happy. This is not a cause for concern, since the overwhelming majority of human beings are intelligent enough to be happier. What most people lack are:

1. The awareness that what will make them happy demands a great deal of thought

2. The self-discipline to overcome their natural inclination to do what is most pleasurable at the moment rather than what is most happiness-inducing

3. The wisdom to consistently answer the question "Will *this* make me happier or unhappier?"

This book offers advice for dealing with all three of these challenges.

Chapter 4

There Is No Good Definition of Happiness

I offer no definition of happiness.

It may seem odd that an author has written a book on a subject that he cannot define, yet I have done so, and it is not odd. If it seems strange, it is because our scientific age demands that we provide definitions, measurements, and statistics in order to be taken seriously. Yet most of the important things in life cannot be precisely defined or measured. Can we define or measure love, beauty, friendship, or decency, for example?

For those who insist on a definition, here are dictionary definitions of the word *happy*:

1. Characterized by good luck; fortunate

2. Enjoying, showing, or marked by pleasure, satisfaction, or joy

3. Being especially well-adapted

4. Cheerful

Does this help? I don't think so. Therefore, instead of defining happiness, I propose two other ways to understand the subject of this book. One is to paraphrase the U.S. Supreme Court justice who, addressing the issue of obscenity, said, "I cannot define it, but I know it when I see it." In discussing happiness, we do not need to be scientifically precise or to provide evidence that would hold up in court. I have never defined happiness in any of my lectures, and it has never seemed to inhibit dialogue on the subject. Members of the audience and I all knew what we were discussing, however any of us might define it.

The other way to more precisely explain the subject, or at least the intent, of *Happiness Is a Serious Problem* is by focusing on *unhappiness*. Although we may never be able to define happiness, and its full attainment may forever be elusive, most of us do think we understand unhappiness and very much intend to avoid it. *Happiness Is a Serious Problem* may therefore be understood as intending to reduce unhappiness just as much as to provide happiness.

Chapter 5

Life Is Tragic

I do not come to the subject of happiness from a particularly rosy outlook on life. On the contrary, I come to it from a largely tragic view of life. I believe that suffering is real, not as some fine souls in the East would have it, a function of the ego, and not as some fine souls in the West would have it, "all for the best." Some suffering is a result of egocentrism, and sometimes suffering does indeed lead to positive results, but much suffering that people have had to endure is undeserved, awful, and leads to nothing positive. (I believe in an afterlife, but this book is written about achieving happiness in this life.)

I also believe in the reality of evil. It is not merely "the absence of good," it is a genuine horror unto itself, and I have spent much of my life studying it. I have written *Happiness Is a Serious Problem* with constant awareness of the Nazi gas chambers, the Communist gulags, the almost universal horrors of racism, and the daily news reports of vicious crime and terrorism.

There are a number of important philosophical and emotional consequences to having such an outlook. For one thing, I walk around amazed at my good fortune. Given how much unjust suffering and unhappiness there are, I am deeply grateful for, sometimes even perplexed by, how much misery I have been spared. For another, given my view that tragedy is normal, *I try to be happy unless something happens that makes me unhappy, rather than unhappy unless something makes me happy.* Most people go through life waiting for something wonderful to happen to them to make them happy. My attitude is that so long as nothing terrible is happening to us, we ought to be happy. Finally, this tragic view of life leads me to have little patience with the chronic complaining I hear in modern society from people who have so much yet act as if life and society have conspired to oppress them.

Moreover, life has much pain built into it even for people who lead inordinately blessed lives. Even in the best instance (i.e., a long and healthy life), we all experience the awful sadness of death—whether ours or that of loved ones. We all leave behind so much unfinished emotional and other business. And in life itself, all of us experience, in author Judith Viorst's inimitable words, a series of very painful "necessary losses." For example, as I write these words, my youngest child, Aaron, is nearing his fifth birthday. My wife and I rejoice at his growing up, yet there is a lump of sadness in both of us as we watch these uniquely endearing early years disappear forever. Even when life is not tragic, indeed, even when it is good, it surely is bittersweet.

Part II

Major Obstacles to Happiness and How to Deal with Them

Chapter 6

Human Nature

Human Nature Is Insatiable

I once came across a newspaper advertisement that crystallized the problem of happiness for me. The advertisement, which was for a Los Angeles sex therapy clinic, read: "If you are not completely satisfied with your sex life, give us a call." At first, the ad meant nothing to me. But for some reason I felt compelled to think about it. And when I did, it became clear to me that this was a truly brilliant ad: if all the people in Los Angeles who were not completely satisfied with their sex life contacted the clinic, everyone in Los Angeles would contact the clinic.

Why? Because the advertisement used the magic words *completely satisfied*. Who is completely satisfied with anything? To illustrate this point, imagine these ads:

"If you are not completely satisfied with your income, give us a call."

"If you are not completely satisfied with your spouse, give us a call."

"If you are not completely satisfied with your children, give us a call."

"If you are not completely satisfied with your parents, give us a call."

"If you are not completely satisfied with your toothpaste, give us a call."

We are completely satisfied with nothing.

The reason is human nature. It is insatiable—and that is why no single obstacle to happiness is greater than human nature. Whatever our nature desires—love, sex, money, attention, pleasure, food, security—cannot be supplied in sufficient quantities to satisfy it completely.

Pay attention to the order of words first spoken by a child, and you will probably notice what I did with my youngest. His first word was *Mama*. Then came *Dada*. And his third word was *more*. These words of a baby accurately represent our deepest urges—first for love and security and then for more—of everything.

That human nature is the greatest single obstacle to happiness is too rarely pointed out by those who speak or write about happiness. First, it strikes many people as too pessimistic. Second, citing our own nature as the greatest obstacle to happiness means that to be happy, we have to battle ourselves, and this is not something many people want to hear. Third, it undermines the common desire to attribute one's unhappiness to outside forces.

Nevertheless, whether we wish to confront it or not, human nature is the greatest obstacle to happiness, and that is why this book directs so much attention to the battle we must wage with ourselves to achieve a happier life.

What to Do with the Insatiability of Human Nature

Our Brain, Not Our Nature, Must Determine Our Happiness

Because human nature is insatiable, our brain, with its rational and philosophical abilities, not our nature, must be the arbiter of whether we are happy. We must be able, in effect, to tell our nature that although we hear it and respect it, our mind, not our nature, will determine whether we are satisfied.

First, can we decide to be satisfied with what we have? A poor man who can make himself satisfied with his portion will be happier than a wealthy man who does not allow himself to be satisfied with his portion.

Second, if we are not satisfied with what we have, will we allow that dissatisfaction to make us unhappy? *Unhappiness* does not necessarily follow from *dissatisfaction*. A person may not be able or may simply choose not to be satisfied—and still not necessarily be unhappy. Just as we can usually choose whether to be dissatisfied, we can usually choose whether to allow dissatisfaction to make us unhappy.

I am not sure which way is better or more mature—is it better to talk yourself into being satisfied, or is it better, or at least nobler, to acknowledge your dissatisfaction and then not allow it to make you unhappy?

I usually prefer the latter approach. We should be able to say to ourselves, "I can be happy with what I have even though I am not satisfied with it." This enables us to do two things:

1. Maintain awareness of what we are feeling while not allowing it to sabotage our happiness

2. Work on reducing whatever it is that causes us dissatisfaction

Distinguish Between Dissatisfactions

There is another way to deal with the omnipresence of dissatisfaction: distinguish between two types of dissatisfactions—necessary and unnecessary.

One example of necessary dissatisfaction is the dissatisfaction that all creative people have regarding their work. This is necessary dissatisfaction because it helps to ensure that the creative person will constantly strive to improve that work. Such dissatisfaction should therefore not lead to unhappiness. We need it to improve our lives.

To cite an example of necessary dissatisfaction in the personal realm, my wife is often dissatisfied with the level of communication in our marriage. In her view, we could almost always be more open and honest about our feelings and spend more time together. While she is happy in our marriage, her dissatisfaction with the level of our communication ensures ever greater intimacy and therefore a better marriage. (Even her husband, who is usually rather satisfied with the level of their communication, acknowledges this.)

Unnecessary dissatisfaction is dissatisfaction over either what is unimportant or what is important but unchangeable. To cite an example of dissatisfaction over the unimportant, I am always somewhat dissatisfied with the quality of my stereo system, no matter how good it really is. I know, however, that even if I were to own a bad stereo system, I would not be so foolish as to allow the poor quality of a stereo system to diminish my happiness. (On the other hand, I do allow a great system to increase my happiness, since I will increase happiness whenever possible.) The key to dissatisfaction not making you unhappy is to know which dissatisfaction is over the important (e.g., the level of marital intimacy) and which dissatisfaction is over the unimportant. Once you do, you can actually retain dissatisfaction over the unimportant and even have fun with it—I immensely enjoy constantly searching for better stereo equipment.

The second source of unnecessary dissatisfaction is dissatisfaction over the unchangeable—even if what is unchangeable *is* important. It takes great strength and wisdom to be able to recognize that dissatisfaction over what cannot be changed is ultimately unnecessary dissatisfaction. Your dissatisfaction may be an entirely valid one, but if its cause cannot be changed, it only increases unhappiness. The well-known Twelve-Step prayer puts this best: "God, grant me the serenity to accept the things I cannot change, the courage to change the things I can, and the wisdom to know the difference." Only when you have the serenity to accept the things you cannot change will you recognize that the dissatisfaction you feel over them is indeed unnecessary.

Why Were We Created with an Insatiable Nature?

If, indeed, human nature is insatiable and therefore the greatest obstacle to happiness, why was our nature so created? It would seem that either nature or God played a rather malicious trick on us.

Not only was no trick played on us, it is actually a great blessing that human nature cannot be satisfied. If it were in our nature to be fully satisfied, we would have no motivation to accomplish anything in either the worldly or the personal realm. Human dissatisfaction with disease has led to cures for illnesses; dissatisfaction with limitations has led to our inventions; dissatisfaction with previous aesthetic expression has motivated great works of art; and, of course, dissatisfaction with the moral state of society has led to moral improvements in it, from the abolition of slavery to the creation of democracy. In the personal realm, human dissatisfaction is what makes personal improvement possible, whether it be better emotional ties to others, better personal ethics, or better personal health. Indeed, anything that becomes better does so as a result of previous dissatisfaction.

Thank God for dissatisfaction. It is a distinguishing and ennobling human trait. There is no reason to believe that animals have it. Give animals their food, shelter, and security and they will be contented. Give these things to human beings, and the next moment they want more of each and are dissatisfied with something else. Complete satisfaction is not available to people.

The matriarch of modern dance, Martha Graham, put the necessity of dissatisfaction best: "No artist is pleased. There is no satisfaction whatever at any time. There is only a queer, divine dissatisfaction; a blessed unrest that keeps us marching and makes us more alive than the others." Cherish human dissatisfaction, but do not let it make you unhappy.

Chapter 7

Comparing Ourselves
with Others

How do we know if we are happy? This would seem to be an easily answered question—we are happy when we feel happy. But if feelings alone determined our level of happiness, we could honestly say that we were happy at 1 o'clock, unhappy at 2:30, happy again at 3:30, and so on all through the day. Obviously this is neither an accurate nor a productive way of assessing our happiness.

But if feelings alone do not determine whether we are happy, what does? The answer, for most people, is to compare themselves with others—which would not be a problem if people compared themselves with *most* other people. But they do not. Most people compare themselves with very few people—those they think are happier than they are.

For example, do you compare your income with that of people who make less than you or people who make more? I recall reading that an actor who receives millions of dollars for every film was unhappy because Arnold Schwarzenegger was making a few million more. Had this actor compared his salary with that of, let us say, any of his high school classmates, he would have been deliriously happy at his extraordinary good fortune. Instead he chose to compare his income with that of one of the few actors in the world who makes more than he does.

That is why a less than noble part of me gets a perverse joy each year when *Forbes* magazine lists the 400 wealthiest Americans. I imagine that some of these people walk around throughout the year quite impressed with their wealth. Then, before all the world, the truth comes out—they are only number 268! I suspect that many of these people are quite unhappy when this issue of *Forbes* appears—it reminds them and the rest of the world how many people are in fact wealthier than they are. Of course, for those who do not assess their happiness by comparing themselves with those who they think are happier—or, as in this case, comparing their wealth with that of those who earn more—this issue of *Forbes* is irrelevant. Whatever their ranking in wealth, they know that they are among the world's most materially fortunate people.

You don't have to be listed in *Forbes* to suffer from comparing yourself with people you think are happier than you are. Most of us do it. For example, many people compare their lives with the lives of famous people such as movie stars—and then envy their presumed happiness.

As common a practice as this may be, it is profoundly mistaken. How many stars' memoirs have to be written before people realize how few of them are happy? Indeed, many of these memoirs reveal lives of greater unhappiness than the average reader's life. Yet most readers do not draw the important conclusion—that people with fame, fortune, and glamour are often quite miserable because fame, fortune, and glamour are not vehicles to happiness. Instead, most readers conclude that the author of each memoir had a particularly tough life. Then these readers go on to compare their lives with that of another glamorous person—until that person writes his or her unhappy memoirs.

Comparing ourselves with people we think are happier than we are is not confined to comparing ourselves with the rich and famous. People compare themselves with anyone they think is happier. It can be a cousin, an acquaintance, or most often, someone we barely know. In fact, the less we know about the people with whom we compare ourselves, the more dramatic the difference in assumed happiness. In the inimitable words of Helen Telushkin, philosopher, homemaker, and mother of my friend the writer Joseph Telushkin, "The only happy people I know are people I don't know well."

This observation is a one-sentence antidote to this obstacle to happiness. If all of us realized that the people with whom we negatively compare our happiness are plagued by pains and demons of which we know little or nothing, we would stop comparing our happiness with others'. Think of those people you know well, and you will realize the truth of Helen Telushkin's comment. Most likely you know how much unhappiness everyone you know well has experienced. And even with regard to these people whom you know well, chances are that you do not know with what inner demons—emotional, psychological, economic, sexual, or related to alcohol or drugs—they have to struggle.

I recall meeting a young radio talk show host during my last book tour. He struck me as particularly successful, healthy, and happy. He spoke to me of his love for his beautiful wife (whose photo adorned his studio), his love for his young daughters, and his joy at being a talk show host in a major city where he loved living. Because none of it sounded contrived, I remember falling into the trap of thinking that he might be one of those fortunate few people for whom everything seemed to have gone right. Then we started talking about our mutual love of computers, and the discussion moved to the Internet. He blessed its existence, he told me, because he could look up so much information on multiple sclerosis—the terrible disease afflicting his young wife.

I felt like a fool, having violated my own rule and assumed that little unhappiness existed in this man's life.

In daily life, most of us put on a problem-free demeanor. "How are things?" we are asked. "Fine" or even "Great" (hyperbole is not rare among Americans) is our automatic response, as it usually ought to be. Few of us really want to hear the problems afflicting everyone to whom we say, "How are you?" (One old witticism defines a pest as

23

someone who when asked "How are you?" answers honestly.) But we pay a price for everyone's putting on a happy face—we start believing that life for everyone else *is* great.

I wonder what effect it must have had on our assumptions about others' happiness when we started smiling every time we were photographed. When I look at old photos, I am struck by how few people smiled for the camera. It apparently didn't occur to most people back then that they had to look happy in every photograph. Given the hardships of life, they probably would have found it silly to "smile on the count of three."

The negative effects of always putting on a happy face can be illustrated by a situation I often imagine: Two couples leave their homes to meet for dinner at a restaurant. Couple A have a big fight on the way to dinner, as do couple B. But when the two couples finally arrive at the restaurant, they all act as if everything is fine.

"Hi, how are you two doing?" they both ask one another.

"Fine, great. And how are you two?" they both reply.

During dinner neither couple utter a word about their fight. Driving home, couple A say to each other, "Did you see couple B— how happy and in love they are? Why can't we be that happy?" Meanwhile in their car, couple B are saying the exact same thing: "Did you see couple A—how happy and in love they are? Why can't we be that happy?"

Not only were the couples unhappy from their respective fights, they are now even more unhappy as a result of comparing themselves with the other couple! They suffer from what can be called compound unhappiness—just as compound interest is interest on interest, compound unhappiness is unhappiness over being unhappy. Such are the dangers of comparing ourselves with others.

The Importance of Intimacy

The unhappiness of these two couples was not only unnecessarily compounded by comparing themselves with the other couple; even their original unhappiness over their fighting could have been reduced. How?

Had the two couples not put on a happy act and opened up to each other, each couple would have left the restaurant happier than when they entered it. All one couple had to do was respond to "How are you guys doing?" with something like, "We're all right, but boy, did we have a fight right before coming here tonight." The odds are overwhelming that if these couples were at all close, the other couple would have responded, "You did? We did too!"

Then, instead of acting as if nothing had happened and everything was wonderful, the couples would be free, thanks to one couple telling the truth, to talk about their respective fights. And if the fights were within the normal range of marital arguments, opening up and finding out that virtually every couple has fights, often about the same things, would have brought everyone closer together. In fact, much marital grief would be avoided if married people talked about their marriages to other married people. In most cases, learning that virtually every marriage has its share of problems, many of which are universal, and then talking—even joking—about them lead to a genuine reduction in marital stress.

There is, in short, no area of life where our happiness would not be increased by ceasing to compare ourselves with people whom we almost always imagine to be happier.

Chapter 8

Images

As self-destructive as comparing ourselves with others is, it may actually be less of an obstacle to happiness than an even more frequent comparison we make—to images.

From childhood on, nearly all of us have images of how our lives should be. It might be an image of our work—how successful, famous, or affluent we will be; or an image of our spouse—how sexy a wife or how wealthy and loving a husband we will have; or an image of our children—how happy and loving they will be. Of course, we may have all three images and many more.

The problem, of course, is that only in rare cases do people's spouses, work, or children live up to their images. Images, after all, are perfect, and life is not.

The Unhappiness Formula: U = I − R

So powerful are these images that you can almost measure your unhappiness by the difference between your images and your reality. In mathematical terms, the formula for measuring many people's unhappiness is therefore $U = I - R$. The amount of Unhappiness equals Images minus Reality.

For example, images are a major source of men's "midlife crisis." By a certain age many men realize that what they have achieved professionally falls short of the image they had of what they would achieve by that age. The difference between the two forms much of that "crisis."*

The solution to this problem of images is inherent in the formula. If unhappiness is measured by the difference between your image and your reality, unhappiness can be reduced by either dropping your images and celebrating your reality or keeping your images and changing your reality.

I cannot give a general rule for which is preferable. Sometimes we have to change our reality; sometimes our reality need not, or cannot, be changed, only celebrated or at least made peace with.

A personal example may help. To the best of my knowledge when I was growing up, no one in my extended family had ever divorced. So I grew up and got married believing that you marry for life. Along with this image of family life came others—of a wife who loved me and whom I loved and of four children seated around the dinner table talking about elevated subjects.

The older I got, the more powerful these images became. So when after five years of marriage, at the age of thirty-seven, I got divorced—with a three-year-old child, no less—my personal world caved in. Everything I had imagined was destroyed—the intact couple, the everlasting love, the four happy children. As a divorced man, I was now a failure in my own eyes. Furthermore, instead of having four happy

---

*Interestingly, women are rarely said to have a midlife crisis. I think that there are two primary reasons for this. One is that women generally do not bank their identity on achievement as much as men do—not being president of something does not cause depression in most women. The other reason is that women tend to have a whole-life crisis. This is not meant critically. Given women's generally more in-tune-with-reality nature, it is not surprising that they would be plagued throughout life with feelings that men don't tend to confront until their middle years.

children, I had but one child and one to whom I was very afraid I was bequeathing unhappiness, not happiness.

Two years later I remarried, and shortly thereafter I confided to my wife, Fran, that I could not shake my unhappy feelings about my family situation. She asked me what was wrong with the family I had (Fran, her daughter, and my son). The truth was, I told her, that aside from the pain of being with my son only half the time, our family life was wonderful. "Then why don't you celebrate it?" she asked.

That is exactly what I decided to do. But I could do so only after deciding to get rid of the images that had prevented me from celebrating what was eminently worthy of celebration—the family I now had. As these words are written, our two children have grown to be happy and good people and we have a third child together. We have all been very fortunate—but if I hadn't dropped those images, I never would have been able to fully appreciate how good—indeed, happy—my family situation was.

I should have known better. I had actually seen the power of images to make a person unhappy much earlier. When I was in my twenties, I met a thirty-five-year-old Orthodox Jewish bachelor whose bachelor status intrigued me. For one thing, religious bachelors of his age are rare—in all religions, adherents to the faith are supposed to marry early so as to confine their sexual behavior to marriage. For another, he complained bitterly about how lonely he was and how much he ached to be married.

"So why aren't you married?" I asked him.

"Because I haven't met the right woman," he replied earnestly.

I didn't let him get away with that answer.

"Can you describe what 'the right woman' would be like?" I persisted.

"I certainly can," he answered emphatically. "I know exactly what I want—a Playboy Playmate who studies Torah."

Truth to tell, the image of a Playboy centerfold who studied Torah excited me too, but even in my early twenties I knew that the image was more hilarious than realistic. Nevertheless, this man allowed himself to remain lonely and unmarried—because of an image. If he dropped this image, he probably found a wonderful wife, but if he did not drop it, he is undoubtedly to this day a single man. One can only guess at the magnitude of the number of people who deprive themselves of some happiness because they await the perfect happiness that only the realization of an image can provide.

I relate his and my stories because they made me realize how powerful, and therefore how potentially destructive, images are. In my case, dropping my images and embracing my reality worked. In other instances, however, I have worked on changing my reality—as when I left a prestigious but unhappy job—and that also has worked.

Their destructive capabilities notwithstanding, images can sometimes play a very constructive role—especially in emotionally broken lives. When used properly, they can inspire people and give them direction to improve their lives. A psychiatrist related a story of a patient whose mother was pathologically close to him, dressing him in effeminate outfits and babying him. She was married to a man who had to work away from home for long stretches and who came home but twice a month for a few days each time.

When her husband—the patient's father—did come home, the parents would go out nearly all the time to be alone with each other, and they left their son at a movie theater. There he watched movies all day long and was, in the psychiatrist's words, "raised by Cary Grant, Spencer Tracy, and Jimmy Stewart." Later, in high school, because he had no other male role models, he chose friends based on who had the best relationships with their fathers. He constantly surrounded himself with good images of men in life and in films. (Today, unfortunately, films provide few such male images, and society provides children with fewer real-life father images.) Thanks in large part to those images, this man became highly successful both professionally and in fathering his own son.

Though it is not always easy to distinguish between helpful and harmful images, much of the time we can. The religious bachelor's reality was not happy, in large part because of images that prevented him from leading a happier life (i.e., getting married). On the other hand, for the young man whose mother treated him like a girl and whose father had emotionally abandoned him, images were a lifeline to a better life.

Images Can Wreak Havoc in Society

The greatest destruction wrought by images has been in the social realm. Although images of perfection in people's personal lives can cause unhappiness, images of perfect *societies*—utopian images—can cause monstrous evil. In fact, forcefully changing society to conform to societal images was the greatest cause of evil in the twentieth century.

Just as comparing our personal reality to images often wreaks havoc with the decent but imperfect life that we lead, comparing society to some perfect image often leads to making a worse society. The Communists who imagined a utopian Russia destroyed the terribly flawed Czarist society but produced a far worse place and gave us the gulag. The Germans who compared the flawed democracy of Weimar Germany to images of a Great Reich destroyed that imperfect democracy and gave the world Auschwitz. In the Middle East today, some religious people who compare their flawed societies to images of a religious utopia governed by God and their religion's laws support the creation of religious totalitarian states. Americans who compare their society, one of the most just in human history, to a society free of all competition, racism, sexism, and any other real or imagined flaw—or to an imagined idyllic past—often weaken that society by condemning and reforming it excessively and unjustly.

On the other hand, without any images of a better society, we would have little reason to hope for a better world, and we would have little guidance in what to strive for. But images are like fire and need to be handled accordingly.

Chapter 9

The Missing Tile Syndrome

One of human nature's most effective ways of sabotaging happiness is to look at a beautiful scene and fixate on whatever is flawed or missing, no matter how small.

This tendency is easily demonstrated. Imagine looking up at a tiled ceiling from which one tile is missing—you will most likely concentrate on that missing tile. In fact, the more beautiful the ceiling, the more you are likely to concentrate on the missing tile and permit it to affect your enjoyment of the rest of the ceiling.

Now when it comes to ceilings or anything else that can exist in a complete form, concentrating on missing details can be desirable. We don't want a physician to overlook the slightest medical detail or a builder to overlook a single tile. But what is desirable or even necessary in the physical world can be very self-destructive when applied to the emotional world. *Ceilings can be perfect, but life cannot.* In life, there will always be tiles missing—and even when there aren't, we can always *imagine* a more perfect life and therefore *imagine* that something is missing.

This unhappiness-making tendency to focus on what is missing was brought home to me on two occasions. The first was when a bald man confided to me, "Whenever I enter a room, all I see is hair." Poor fellow. When he is around people, all he sees is the hair on other men's heads, and when he looks into the mirror, all he sees is a bald head. Little does he realize how little his baldness means to most others. He was shocked to learn that those of us who have all our hair don't concentrate on, indeed some of us don't even notice, which men are balding. If after meeting five men I were asked which of them was bald, I would be hard pressed to recall.

Most of us who have our hair don't think that having hair is nearly as important to our happiness as the bald man thinks it is. The validity of our perception can be ascertained by investigating whether men with hair are happier than bald men. I do not know whether such a study has been made, but I doubt that there is a correlation between hair and happiness—and if there is, it is a direct result of bald men attributing too much importance to their missing hair and *allowing* it to make them unhappy.

The Missing Tile syndrome is ubiquitous. If you are overweight, all you see are flat stomachs and perfect physical specimens. If you have pimples, all you see is flawless skin. Women who have difficulty getting pregnant walk around seeing only pregnant women and babies. Nor do you need to be overweight, have pimples, be balding, or want a child to believe that you have a missing tile. You can allow any real—or merely perceived—flaw to diminish your happiness.

The second occasion came earlier. I first learned about the Missing Tile syndrome from my friend Joseph Telushkin. We were both single into our thirties, and we often talked about dating and women. The most recurring theme was our—especially my—search for the Most Important Trait in a Woman (MITIAW). I was obsessed with figuring out the MITIAW. Typically after a date I would call Joseph to announce what the MITIAW really was. After one date it would be personality, after another it was physical attractiveness, after another it was intelligence, and after yet another it was good values.

"Joseph," I would say with great certitude, "tonight I finally came to realize the most important thing to look for in a woman." And I would announce what it was.

One night, after years of this foolish search, Joseph opened my eyes. I was about to tell him what the MITIAW was when he stopped me. "Dennis," he interrupted, "don't tell me. I know exactly what you'll say."

"How can you possibly know?" I asked. "You don't even know the woman I was out with."

"It doesn't matter," he replied. "You're about to announce that the Most Important Trait in a Woman is whatever trait tonight's date didn't have."

I was embarrassed at how right he was. I immediately realized that for years I had been declaring that the MITIAW was whatever trait I perceived as missing in the woman I was dating. No wonder I wasn't finding a woman to marry. Since no human being can possess every good trait, every woman, by definition, was missing the Most Important Trait in a Woman! If I truly wanted to find and value a woman, I was in a permanently self-destructive cycle.

We often proclaim whatever we think is missing in another person to be the Most Important Trait. A trait that we believe—or that is in fact—missing in our child becomes the Most Important Trait in a Child. A trait we perceive as missing in our spouse becomes the Most Important Trait in a Husband or Wife. And to make things worse, we then find this trait in other people's children or spouses.

This is yet another way in which we make ourselves, not to mention others, miserable. It is human nature to concentrate on what is missing and deem it the Most Important Trait. Unless we teach ourselves to concentrate on what we *do* have, we will end up obsessing over missing tiles and allow them to become insurmountable obstacles to happiness.

What to Do?

To effectively deal with the Missing Tile syndrome, it is necessary to:

1. Acknowledge how powerful the missing tile perception may be in your life.

2. Identify as precisely as possible what that missing tile is. This enables you to gain clarity about what—or at least what you think—is troubling you.

3. Determine whether having this tile is central to your happiness—or whether it is but another one of your insatiable longings. If your missing tile, to cite a silly example, is a great car, then you can be assured you are suffering from the Missing Tile syndrome, not truly suffering from a missing tile.

Get It, Forget It, or Replace It

Once you have determined what your missing tile is and whether acquiring it will really make you happy, you should do one of three things: get it, forget it, or replace it with a different tile. If you do not do one of these three things, you will allow the missing tile to make you unhappy.

If the tile is not crucial to your happiness, the best solution is to forget it. Life presents too many real obstacles to happiness to allow yourself to be troubled by insignificant ones. If, on the other hand, the tile that is missing is crucial to your happiness, of course try to obtain it. If you cannot, the next best choice is to try to replace it with a different tile that will satisfy you, though presumably not as much as the actual tile. If neither of these options is workable, do everything you can to forget about it and concentrate on the tiles in your life that are not missing.

Get It A few years into my second marriage, though I was happily married and loved our two children (a daughter, Anya, from my wife's previous marriage and a son, David, from mine) and my professional life was also going well, I deeply felt that something important was missing from my life. I wanted another child. There were excellent reasons not to have another child: my wife and I were in our mid-forties, we already had two children, and we loved travel, independence, and freedom. But I could not let go of this missing tile. As hard as I tried to forget about it and concentrate on other passions, this absent tile continued to loom over me. And I was right in identifying it as such. From the day our son Aaron was born, I have not felt a missing tile of any significance.

I was extremely fortunate. I could actually identify and then find my missing tile. For many people this is not possible. In such cases they have to choose either to forget it or replace it. In my case replacing the child-tile with other tiles/passions would have been the second best option. For example, my wife and I could have focused more on each other, spent even more time with our first two children, and directed more energy and attention to work.

Forget It   Another personal example will illustrate the second option—to forget about the missing tile. When I divorced, my oldest son was three years old, and his mother and I agreed to joint physical custody. From the beginning this seemed to work for David, and eleven years later I think I can say that it has worked. But there has never been a time when David's leaving me for his time with his mother was not painful. This was a true missing tile in my life—not being with David every day. And unlike the example above, in this instance it was clear that this tile could not be found. I therefore had to stop thinking—to forget—about the time I didn't have with David and spend as much time as I could with him during the time I did have with him. Ironically, I may well have ended up spending more time with him than if he were always with me.

Replace It   Everyone, consciously or not, has replaced something missing with something else. I think, for example, of Leon Fleisher, one of the greatest pianists of the twentieth century. Early in his career, he was struck with a mysterious affliction that made it impossible for him to play with his right hand. Because the greatest physicians were powerless to help him, he changed his career to teaching, conducting, and playing piano pieces written for the left hand. Perhaps all of these replacements did not bring him the satisfaction that playing with both hands had brought him, but they were infinitely superior to dwelling on his missing right hand.

Chapter 10

Equating Happiness
with Success

One of the most common obstacles to happiness is the equation of happiness with success. Although this equation particularly afflicts men, it has come to afflict many professional women as well.

There are two simple and effective ways to demonstrate that the equation of happiness with success is a mistake.

First, write down what level of success you believe will make you happy. Is it, for example, becoming chief executive officer of a company? Earning three times what you now earn? Owning a business? Becoming a best-selling author? I have found that when people are invited to write down the specific success that will make them happy, many of them begin to realize that whatever level of success they imagine would not make all that much difference in their level of happiness.

They know that whatever success they achieve, shortly after reaching it they will imagine yet a higher level of success. *If you equate happiness with success, you will never achieve the amount of success necessary to make you happy.* There is always more success that can be achieved. Identifying success with happiness is like moving the goalposts back 10 yards every time your football team has a first down—your team may be more and more successful, but the goalposts will always remain unreachable. For success to affect your happiness, you have to be able to say, "I am now successful" (i.e., "I have reached the goalposts"). You may, of course, continue to seek more success but not as a condition necessary for you to be happy.

A second way to demonstrate that success does not equal happiness is to talk to highly successful people and find out if they are happy. I have talked with a number of such people and have found that those who are happy were happy before they were successful—though their success may certainly have added to their happiness. Similarly, those who were unhappy before achieving success are still unhappy. In fact, they are actually unhappier than when they started out. Because they continue to equate happiness with success yet have not achieved happiness, they devote even more time to pursuing even more success. Therefore they do not devote time to doing those things that really would make them happier.

Why Is Success Important to You?

A third reason success does not equal happiness lies in why we pursue it. If success is very important to you, it is essential to discover why.

There are, to be sure, healthy reasons for wanting to enjoy success. It is healthy to want some of the material trappings of success—especially financial security for yourself and your family. It is healthy to want some recognition for your achievements. It is healthy to value the work you do and to want to be successful at it.

However, if you want success because you think your happiness depends on it, or if you think your happiness depends on having ever increasing amounts of money and recognition, this is unhealthy and not at all conducive to happiness. It behooves you to find out why you are so driven. Only then will you be able to recognize why success alone will not make you happy and to free yourself from relentlessly pursuing it.

If you ask yourself, "Why do I want success?" you may learn some interesting things about yourself. For example, many highly successful people have pursued success because their parent(s) gave them love only when they were successful. They have therefore pursued success to make themselves lovable. This is one reason, incidentally, why it is foolish to envy all successful people—many of them are driven by demons that no amount of success can assuage.

For some other highly successful people, professional success functions like a drug: it is pursued in ever increasing doses to medicate pain (hence the appropriateness of the term *workaholic*); it is as unlikely to bring long-term relief; and it brings misery when not available. One example is the actor who lives for applause and shrivels when it is absent.

The Role of Work in Happiness

Success at work cannot be equated with happiness, but work can still be a major source of happiness—if the work is joyful and meaningful.

These two conditions are often not met by the work of those considered very successful. When a person engages in work primarily to make money and achieve success, the work is rarely joyful or ultimately meaningful to the person. This is why unpaid volunteers can easily derive more happiness from their work than millionaires do from theirs. A simple test to ascertain how much you enjoy and derive meaning from your work is to ask yourself whether you would continue doing it if you won the lottery.

I have certainly found this rule applicable to my own work. That which has brought me the greatest success has not brought me the greatest happiness; and that which has brought me the most happiness has not been particularly successful.

My greatest professional success has come from my work as a radio talk show host, which began in 1982. Especially since I began broadcasting on a daily basis, it has brought me some fame and a good income. The radio work that brought me the most happiness, however, was a show that was broadcast only once a week, late on a Sunday night, which provided little fame and paid only a few hundred dollars per show. But every week for ten years I looked forward to doing *Religion on the Line,* a program in which I was the moderator among a Protestant minister, a Roman Catholic priest, a Jewish rabbi, and often a representative of a fourth faith. I love talking about religion, I loved broadening my horizons by meeting representatives of virtually every faith in the world, and I knew that I was doing good work in making religion intellectually alive for about a hundred thousand people each week. I also made lasting friendships, vastly deepened my understanding of religion, grew a great deal by becoming far more open to recognizing that there are many ways to God and holiness, and had great fun—quite a potent combination for increasing happiness.

I left that show to do a prime-time daily three-hour talk show with an audience of half a million people. The ability to influence far more people has been a great source of satisfaction, and the income is very helpful for the breadwinner of a family of five. But the truth is that in terms of work, I was happier doing the less prestigious, less lucrative, less "successful" show, *Religion on the Line.*

Likewise, in my writing career I have derived particular happiness from writing and publishing my own newsletter for the past thirteen years. Though it has never had as many as ten thousand subscribers and though I derive almost no monetary gain from the time-consuming venture of putting it out twice a month, writing it has been an immense source of happiness.

My third greatest work-source of happiness also brings few rewards in terms of success as it is generally defined—teaching the Bible verse by verse at a Jewish seminary.

My own life and work regularly reinforce my belief that the joy and meaning of one's work, not the level of its success, are the source of happiness.

Money and Happiness

Even if one accepts all my arguments against equating professional and material success with happiness, it is undeniable that money can help increase happiness. There is deep joy to be had from a beautiful home; much relief in being able to afford the education, medical care, and other things you want to give your children; much pleasure from listening to Bach on a great music system; deep satisfaction in being able to travel around the world; and immense peace of mind in not having to worry about financial matters.

Do these potentially major contributions of money to happiness therefore invalidate the argument that success should not be equated with happiness? Not at all. Success is success and happiness is happiness.

But while financial success and happiness must not be equated, the pursuit of financial success is not necessarily destructive to happiness. The pursuit of financial success is destructive when engaged in for its own sake and not for reasons that increase happiness. That is why, as noted earlier, it is imperative to determine why you want success.

If you want financial success for reasons such as those enumerated—greater joy, peace of mind, security for loved ones—financial success can increase your happiness, especially if when you achieve financial peace of mind, you pursue other, deeper goals. If, on the other hand, your desire for money emanates from a constant craving for material things or from a need to impress others or from a desire to be rich simply to be rich, becoming a financial success will not increase and may well decrease your happiness. Because once you attain the status of being rich, you will still be stuck with your original unhappiness and unhealthy desires *and* with the additional problem of no longer being able to fantasize that making money will remove your unhappiness. *Unhappy poor people at least have the fantasy that money will make them happy; unhappy rich people don't even have that.*

It is also imperative to determine what you will have to sacrifice in order to make more money and achieve more success. For many people, making a great deal of money comes at the price of forgoing far more

41

important sources of happiness. For example, if you had to ignore your family, do work you resented, repeatedly compromise your highest values, give up friendships, or endure daily aggravation, becoming a financial success would make you an unhappier, not a happier, person.

Defining Success

When most people think of success they think of professional and material success. It is this type of success that cannot be equated with happiness. There are, however, myriad forms of success that do lead to happiness: success in love, in relationships, in child rearing, in touching others' lives, in becoming deeper, in gaining wisdom, in doing good, and in learning about oneself.

Why, then, do so many people narrowly define success as professional or material achievement? This is a complex question because it goes to the heart of many other aspects of life.

One reason we tend to define success in professional and material terms is the primal motivational force of male-female attraction. Men, in particular, tend to equate happiness with professional and material success because it attracts women. The male desire to attract women is such that if women gave their love and attention to men with great stamp collections, philately would become mankind's chief enterprise. Of course, men have similar power over women's behavior, which is one reason many women equate happiness with being beautiful. Men's valuing of physical attractiveness in women is the counterpart to women's valuing of professional and material success in men.

A second reason for defining success in narrow material terms is again primal—most people have a competitive instinct, a need to show that they are more accomplished or more wealthy than others. This is not a social construct of modern civilization. In the New Guinea highlands, I saw men wearing pig tusks to display their material worth, and women from New Guinea to Hollywood exhibit their wealth through expensive jewelry.

A third reason we tend to define success narrowly is that professional and material success is usually more glamorous than most of the more meaningful types of success. For example, though nearly everyone would acknowledge that having good friends is far more meaningful—and far more important to happiness—than having great professional success, few of us would characterize a man who was moderately successful at work but who had deep and loving friendships as "a great success." At the same time, we routinely call wealthy men successful without knowing whether they have a friend in the world. I do not foresee a worldwide movement to use the term *success* more accurately, though such a movement would in fact greatly increase human happiness. But until we reach such a blessed time, we should forthrightly acknowledge that our current definition of success is more conducive to increasing unhappiness than happiness.

The human being is seduced by much that is ephemeral. If it glitters, we seek it. That this flaw is part of human nature is shown by the tale of the Garden of Eden, regarded by the Western world as a fundamental paradigm of the human condition. Adam and Eve seem to have everything anyone could desire, including immortality. There is only one thing that can destroy all that they have—eating the fruit of the Tree of Knowledge of Good and Evil, which is "beautiful to look at." And so, like all of us (Adam and Eve are Everyman and Everywoman), they eat of the forbidden fruit, thinking that because it is "beautiful to look at" it will increase their happiness.

Beautiful homes, shiny cars, gorgeous clothing, glittering jewelry, and of course attractive men and women are all "beautiful to look at." That is why we pursue material success at the cost of all the things that actually do bring us happiness—because it is seductive and glamorous, and we think (if we think the issue through at all) that it will therefore make us happy. How many men have ignored children and wives, never cultivated deep friendships, never deepened their knowledge and wisdom, never looked into themselves—all things that bring happiness—in pursuit of things that are "beautiful to look at"?

I often recall what clergy of every faith have said to me: "I have been with many men approaching death; and not one has ever said, 'I only regret that I didn't spend more time at the office.'"

Chapter 11

Equating Happiness with Fun

When I first wrote an essay arguing that happiness should not be equated with fun, my son David was seven years old. When he looked at my computer screen and sounded out the title words, "Happiness Isn't Fun," he looked at me utterly confused and said, "It isn't?"

To a child, the notion that fun is distinguishable from happiness is simply inconceivable. As adults, many of us continue to hold on to this belief—which is unfortunate, because equating fun with happiness is a great obstacle to happiness.

Most people believe in this equation: H = nF, or the amount of Happiness equals the $n$umber of Fun experiences. As a friend once told me, "I always assumed that if I could just accumulate enough fun experiences, I'd be happy."

Most people believe that happiness and fun are virtually identical. Ask them, for example, to imagine a scene of happy people. Most people immediately conjure up a picture of people *having fun* (e.g., laughing, playing games, drinking at a party). Few people imagine a couple raising children, a couple married thirty years, someone reading a great book, or people doing any of the other things that really do bring happiness.

Another way to ascertain the importance people attach to fun is to look at one of the few places where people publicly state what is important to them—singles ads. Fun and things that provide fun—skiing, boating, tennis, movies, going to sports events, dining out—overwhelm all other considerations in these ads, which are, it is important to remember, mostly for prospective mates, not for fun-time friends. Fun itself is repeatedly mentioned as necessary in the persons being sought and as a defining characteristic of the person who took out the ad.

The following ads are all taken from just one issue of *New York* magazine, probably home to the most sophisticated singles ads in America; they cost an average of hundreds of dollars per entry (italics are mine).

- Handsome man in early 30's, looking for . . . a *fun*, romantic relationship.

- Attractive, Long Island, vivacious . . . seeks loving white male, 45–55, for sincere *fun*. [What is *insincere* fun?]

- Jewish male, 45, optometrist looking for someone to share *boating, skiing, and fun* relationship. [Just in case boating and skiing alone do not make it clear how important fun is to our optometrist, he adds "fun relationship."]

- Long curly hair, pretty, professional, *fun*.

- Highly successful, highly attractive, highly educated, *fun-loving* Manhattanite seeking that ultimate male counterpart.

- Exciting woman searching for romantic, *fun-loving* man over 50.

- Attractive, divorced white female, 41, seeking a *fun-loving*, sensitive white male.

- Attractive, spirited, single white female who loves sports, cooking, travel, and *having fun*.

- You're a successful professional man, over 46, with . . . *a flair for fun*.

Finally, a man who is serious about fun:

- Professional, athletic, handsome Christian male, 28, seeks female . . . for *dance, beach, lively fun,* serious only.

Even acknowledging that people who enjoy having fun are preferable as friends and companions to people who don't, the problem of overemphasizing fun remains: Why is fun considered so important? Why this relentless pursuit of fun?

The most obvious reason is that fun is enjoyable, and we are programmed to pursue what we enjoy—sex, food, drink, and all other pleasures of the senses. But there is a deeper reason why people so seriously pursue fun. They believe that it will bring them happiness.

Very often the reason that people reach faulty conclusions is not their inability to reason; it is that they reason from faulty premises. The refusal of ancient seamen to go far out to sea lest they fall off the world was not a function of faulty reasoning; it was, in fact, sound reasoning—based on the faulty premise that the earth was flat. So too, the many people who think that more parties, sex, movies, and clothes, classier cars, and a whole host of other fun-providers will bring them happiness are not using faulty reasoning. The fault lies in their original premise—that more fun will bring happiness.

It is this flawed premise that leads many people to pursue fun with the same seriousness that they pursue professional success. For example, unless my own experiences and those reported to me are atypical, many people attend parties not because they actually have so much fun, let alone become happier, at them but rather because they associate parties with fun and believe that fun leads to happiness.

This is what keeps people returning for more fun-providers that provide no happiness and often not even much fun. If tonight's party wasn't much fun and didn't increase my happiness, it was the wrong party. Next time, with a trendier, more fun-loving, or wealthier group, I will have a great time. Somewhere, this thinking goes, there are people having a great time, and those people are happy.

How Fun and Happiness Differ

To understand why fun doesn't create happiness and can even conflict with it, we must understand the major difference between fun and happiness: *fun is temporary; happiness is ongoing.* Or to put it another way, fun is during, happiness is during and after.

Sex provides a good example. Little in life is as much fun as seducing or being seduced by someone highly desirable and then having exciting sex with that person. Yet most people, if they do not care for that person, are not happier afterward. Casual sex is a good illustration of the fun-is-during, happiness-is-after rule.

To further illustrate the distinction between fun and happiness, I offer three types of fun.

Amusements

The first type of fun is simple amusement such as going to an amusement park, attending a sporting event, or watching a movie or television. While all of these activities are fun, none of them creates happiness. This is not an argument against any of them. Such activities can play a very constructive role in life. When used judiciously, they help us maintain our happiness—by helping us to relax, by deflecting concentration away from our problems, and by enabling us to laugh.

But amusements do not *create* happiness, and they can pose a danger to it. Because the enjoyment of amusements ends when the amusement ends, unhappy people can come to rely on amusements as an escape from unhappiness and constantly pursue them.

Fun That Decreases Happiness

There is a second type of fun, one that can actually decrease happiness. I am not referring to anything either immoral or illegal, such as taking drugs. I am referring to nothing more sinister than, for example, eating fattening food. Eating delicious foods is a great deal

47

of fun, but for many people these foods are more a source of unhappiness than of happiness. Which group is happier—those who have fun eating all the fattening foods they enjoy, or those who have learned to usually deprive themselves of that fun and keep the body they want?

Compulsory Fun

A third type of fun that illustrates the during-versus-after rule is what I call compulsory fun. Its distinguishing feature is that it is induced more by societal expectations than by the individual's desires.

Good examples are New Year's Eve and, for those who have changed holy days into holidays, Christmas. For these people, the purpose of Christmas is to be merry and of New Year's Eve, to have fun. Yet this time of year is notorious for people experiencing increased *unhappiness* both for those who go to the compulsory parties and for those who do not. Those who do not go to Christmas and New Year's Eve parties think they are missing out on the fun that everyone else is having. And those who do attend these parties feel that they must have a great time or else they have wasted New Year's Eve's singular potential for fun. Yet as all the drinking accompanying New Year's Eve suggests, people are hardly increasing their happiness, a fact that many New Year's Eve revelers recognize the next morning.

This is not to suggest that there is something wrong, in terms of either morality or happiness, in attending Christmas, New Year's Eve, or any other parties. It is only to suggest that "compulsory fun" often doesn't deliver the fun that one expects and that it certainly doesn't deliver happiness.

Fun versus Happiness

Fun is most definitely important to a happy life (see below), but unless understood and used properly, it actually reduces happiness.

One reason is that fun shares a number of characteristics with drugs. Motivated by the belief that fun (and its partner, excitement) will bring happiness, many men and women become fun addicts, people who pursue fun with ever increasing amounts of energy, money, and time and sometimes at great cost to personal lives and family.

Fun shares an additional trait with drugs—the next dose must be as strong or stronger than the previous one. For many people, fun is not satisfying in moderate doses; the "kick" is insufficient. And for those who associate fun with happiness, seeking fun in moderation is as absurd as seeking happiness in moderation.

The problem of needing to raise the excitement threshold for fun is a real one. Think of how much fun you had the first time you kissed—merely kissed—a boyfriend or girlfriend. Sometime thereafter kissing ceased to provide enough fun, and heavy petting began. Then its ability to provide enough pleasure wore off too, and intercourse ensued. Then, for those who pursue fun rather than happiness, in time that too loses much of its ability to provide fun and excitement, and more potent pleasures are needed. Examples might include seeking sex with other partners either through infidelity, which usually reduces happiness, or by remaining single and having many partners, a lifestyle associated more with loneliness than with happiness.

In this regard, I sometimes think that Hollywood stars have an almost God-given role to play in our world. The richest, most beautiful, and most famous people, who do indeed have constant access to the most fun—the best parties, the most sex with glamorous partners, the most expensive cars, the most luxurious homes, the most exotic vacations, and the most opportunities to engage in and get to attend the best sports and theatrical events—repeatedly remind us that these things simply do not lead to happiness. As noted earlier, in memoir after memoir they reveal to us the sad lives behind all the fun. We should feel greatly indebted to every Hollywood star who has written about his or her alcoholism, lost children, depressed life, profound loneliness, and various addictions. If we could learn from others' lives—a trait that may best define wisdom—we would be very grateful to these people for providing such credible testimony that fun doesn't lead to happiness.

But because most people do not learn from others' lives, they continue to believe that the next fun-provider will do what the preceding fun-providers have not been able to do—make them happy.

In addition to having druglike qualities, there is another, equally powerful way in which fun can actually decrease happiness. If we identify having fun with happiness, we will identify the opposite of fun, pain, with unhappiness. However, because no happiness is possible without pain, the attempt always to avoid it by having fun as much as possible makes happiness impossible. This is discussed in the next chapter.

The Proper Use of Fun
The Importance of Fun

A life devoted to avoiding fun is no more likely to lead to happiness than a life devoted to having fun. As in every other aspect of life, the middle road is the road to happiness.

A good way to understand the role of fun in happiness is by drawing an analogy to food and spice, with food representing life's basic needs and spice representing fun. We cannot live on spice alone; it is the food that spices make tasty that gives us the nutrition to live. But food without spices renders eating more of a chore than a joy. So too, we cannot live on fun alone, but living solely on the nonfun essentials of life renders life a chore, not a joy.

Understood this way, fun is very important to happiness. Life has a great deal of stress and routine, and human beings need release from them. Fun provides such a release. That is why we are much better able to deal with life's problems after a vacation.

The case on behalf of fun needs to be stated as firmly as the case against equating fun with happiness. Just as there are hedonists, people who live to have as much fun as possible (and therefore do not achieve lasting happiness), there are ascetics, people who oppose having fun, and anhedonics (the opposite of hedonists), people who cannot have fun. They may be ascetic or anhedonic for psychological or philosophical reasons. Such people may have been raised to associate fun with guilt, to believe that fun is sinful or inimical to a truly deep and meaningful life.

How to Use Fun

Keeping the food metaphor in mind, we can say that fun comes in two varieties—spices and dessert. Spices enable people to enjoy eating the foods that are necessary for proper nutrition (e.g., spices can make otherwise bland protein foods delicious). Likewise, the best way to use fun is as something that enables us to enjoy what is necessary for a good and happy life (e.g., work, raising a family, study).

Desserts, on the other hand, are foods that are eaten solely for fun. Just as some fun is analogous to spices, some fun is analogous to desserts. Such fun does not accompany important activity; it is just fun. It is good sometimes just to have fun without any meaningful associated activity, just as it is good sometimes just to have dessert. But a fun-only life is as unfulfilling as dessert-only meals.

Thus, instead of relying on relatively meaningless diversions (desserts) for most of our fun, we should try to make the important things we do as much fun as possible (adding spice to nutrition). For example, I often find writing difficult and laborious and therefore try to make it as much fun as possible. When I write in longhand I use different fountain pens and different colored inks, and when writing with a computer, I periodically change keyboards, alternate fonts, and use the clearest and most colorful monitor I can afford.

Fun can be injected into virtually every pursuit in life. That is where fun's greatest importance lies. If you can have fun while doing what is significant—raising a family, working at your profession, volunteering with the needy—you will truly be a happier person.

Then there is also the time and need for dessert—doing something just for fun. From hobbies to vacations to sports, the possibilities are (sometimes unfortunately) limitless.

Here I want to make a specific recommendation to young readers who seek greater happiness. I know that it is very tempting to use vacation time just to have fun. Yet I feel very fortunate that as a young person I realized that there was an alternative to "fun in the sun," that a vacation can provide not only fun but also personal growth. While many of my friends used their vacations to lie in the sun on a beach or by a hotel pool, I usually spent the same amount of money to travel to some foreign country (unfortunately alone; no one wanted to come with me to Bulgaria, for example). I may not have had as much fun per se as some of my friends did, but my trips were fun *and* they brought me enduring happiness. I consider my travel to more than seventy countries to be among the most life-enhancing things I have ever done.

Conclusion

A proper understanding of fun is one of life's most liberating and powerful discoveries. It liberates our time—now we can spend less time on fun that doesn't make us happy. It can liberate us financially—perhaps we don't really need to buy that expensive item to be happier. It liberates us from envy—we now realize that all those people we think are so happy because they seem to be having so much fun probably aren't.

The moment we understand that fun by itself does not lead to happiness, we begin to lead our lives differently. The effects of this realization are life transforming.

Chapter 12

Fear and Avoidance of Pain

As we have seen, the identification of fun with happiness has many negative consequences. One of its worst consequences is reinforcement of the belief that if you want to be happy, you should avoid pain. After all, if fun leads to happiness, pain must lead to unhappiness.

Nothing could be less true. Everything that leads to happiness involves pain. While it is widely acknowledged that success in professional life and in sports, to cite two examples, is associated with pain (e.g., hard work, self-discipline, delayed gratification), success in happiness is almost never associated with pain.

As a result, many people avoid some of the very things that would bring them the deepest happiness, such as marriage, children, intellectually challenging pursuits, religious commitment, and volunteer work. They fear the pain that inevitably accompanies such things and therefore devote more time to "fun" things that bring little happiness, such as watching television.

As the Psalmist put it millennia ago, "Those who sow in tears will reap in joy." Many people, however, believe that they can both sow and reap without tears.

Ask a forty-year-old bachelor why he stays single even though he admits that dating provides less and less satisfaction (and no happiness), and he will most likely respond that he fears permanent commitment, something that is quite painful to male nature. Yet although the bachelor life is associated with fun and excitement, it is married men, according to every study on the subject, who are happier and who live healthier and longer.

Similarly, couples who choose not to have children are choosing a more painless life than those who choose to have children. But there is a happiness that derives from having children that cannot be duplicated without them (this is discussed in more detail in Chapter 25).

Many people seem to want this epitaph: "I led as painless a life as possible." But the purpose of life is not to avoid pain. That is the purpose of an animal's life—but animals cannot know happiness.

"To live is to suffer," wrote Dostoyevsky. If the great Russian novelist meant that to live is only to suffer, he was too pessimistic. But if he meant that to live and experience life fully one must suffer, he was entirely right.

One reason more than a few members of my generation are unhappy is that they were raised to believe that a pain-free life is possible. Many of their parents worked assiduously to shield their children from pain and frustration, unwittingly teaching them that avoidance of pain is important to happiness and thereby preventing them from learning how to deal with pain.

The choice is yours: do you want as pain-free a life as possible, or do you want as life-filled a life as possible? The two are mutually exclusive. "No pain, no gain" is not only true for developing a good body; it is equally true for developing a good life.

Chapter 13

Expectations

When I studied comparative religion in college, I learned a Buddhist teaching that has had a deep and lasting effect on my life: Pain in life comes from unfulfilled desires and expectations. Based on this understanding, Buddhism aims to do away with both desires and expectations.

I could not accept the first part of the Buddhist goal—ridding oneself of desires. Individuals and societies that attempt to do away with desires often pay a price that I am unwilling to pay. For example, without preserving a desire for health, no one would work to discover cures or vaccines for illnesses. This is one reason that Western society, whose religious and humanistic traditions hold desires to be acceptable, has been the source of most modern medical progress. China, which has also cultivated the medical arts, is also heir to desire-accepting traditions.

Of course, many of our desires are unhealthy and can lead to negative consequences. But desires are an indispensable part of a good (i.e., moral and happy) life, even though they can easily work against happiness.

Expectations, however, are another matter. Here the Buddhist teaching is of universal importance. If we understand expectations to mean certitude that something will happen, that we can take the good we have for granted, or that we can feel entitled to the things we want, then expectations lead to unhappiness, cause gratuitous pain, and undermine the most important source of happiness—gratitude.

Though getting rid of expectations strikes most people as impossible and/or undesirable, minimizing expectations is both realistic and highly desirable. In general, *expectations lead to unhappiness.*

Take the expectation of health. For most people, the only time good health brings them happiness is when they do not expect to be healthy and then find out that they are. Imagine that you discover a strange new lump on your body. You go to a doctor, who tells you that it looks suspicious and that you should have a biopsy. After waiting a week for the results, you learn that the lump is benign. That day will be one of the happiest days of your life.

Now this is remarkable because the day before you discovered the lump you were not one bit healthier than you were on the supremely happy day you learned that your lump was benign. Nothing in the state of your health has changed, yet you are now profoundly happy. Why? Because on this day, *you did not expect* to be healthy.

Am I therefore saying that we should not expect to be healthy? Yes. We can and should *desire* to be healthy and work at being healthy. But ideally, we should awaken every day and be as happy about our good health as if we had just received the wonderful news that a lump was diagnosed as benign.

A second example: The greatest part of the pain we suffer when a loved one dies is usually caused less by the person's death than by expectations unfulfilled—namely, our expecting the person to have lived longer. No matter how much we love our parents, we experience greater pain if they die relatively young than if they die at the age of ninety. We deeply miss loved ones no matter what age they die, but we accept their death with far greater equanimity if it comes at a late age.

For the same reason—different expectations—in centuries past when children often died in their first years, many parents did not grieve as much as parents now do at the early death of a child. Earlier generations of parents *did not expect* their children to live beyond infancy to the same extent as parents do today. Here too it is expectations that are at the root of unhappiness.

A third example: If we expect to get hired for a job, and we don't, we become unhappy. Does this mean that when we go for a job interview, we should not expect to get hired? Yes. But doesn't such an attitude conflict with much of the professional advice about getting jobs? Yes again.

I will explain by way of a personal story. My greatest macro goal has always been to communicate my values and ideas to as many people as possible. So I was terribly excited when, at the age of thirty-two, I was invited to try out for the job of talk show host on one of the most successful talk radio stations in America, KABC in Los Angeles. I can still recall my attitude going into the station. I believed that I deserved the job, I wanted the job, and I had great confidence in my ability to impress my would-be employers. But I did not *expect* to get the job.

Why not? Because I know that I do not fully control my fate. For example, I know the role of luck in life—what if I had laryngitis on the night I tried out? What if the program director's nephew was also applying for the job? What if I had a car accident that night?

This attitude may sound self-defeating to those who believe that professional success is dependent upon always expecting victory. But that is not the case. I wanted that job as much as any applicant, and I suspect that I had as much self-confidence as any applicant. But unlike any candidate for the position who expected to get the job, I spared myself the unhappiness that would have come from not getting it. Furthermore, when I was hired, I experienced immense gratitude largely because I did not have such expectations, surely more gratitude than if I had expected the job.

For most people in most circumstances, expectations are unnecessary impediments to happiness. When expectations are unfulfilled they cause gratuitous pain, and when they are fulfilled, they diminish gratitude, the most important element in happiness.

Expectations Diminish Happiness When They Are Not Met— and When They Are Met

If our expectations are not met, we suffer the pain of disappointment, and the greater the expectation, the greater the pain—needless pain, moreover.

Let's return to expecting the job for which you apply. We are often advised to expect to get the job and assured that this will greatly enhance our chances of getting it. To prove this, we always hear from those who won the job, the prize, the raise, or any other highly sought goal that these winners "always knew" that they would get what they wanted and that this knowing or expecting was instrumental to their success.

The problem with this attitude is that we never hear from the 250 applicants who also expected to win the job but didn't. What pain are these people needlessly suffering because they expected to get a job that they didn't get? We frequently hear the newest Hollywood stars tell us that they "always knew" they would become stars. But the media do not visit the restaurants of Los Angeles to interview the thousands of waiters and waitresses who also "always knew" they would be stars. (Waiting on tables is, of course, an utterly honorable way to make a living, but being a waiter is not the point here. The point is that we never hear about the far more numerous individuals whose expectations are never realized—only from the tiny percentage of "winners.")

For a handful of people, expecting to get a job or to make a sale may sometimes be helpful, but for most people—and even for that handful of people—having expectations is nearly always destructive to happiness. Having expectations may work for the one person in 250 or 10,000 who wins, but it is the road to greater unhappiness for the 249 or 9,999 who do not. It is for all these people—and all of us are sometimes among these people—that I write these words of warning about expectations.

While it is obvious that having expectations increases unhappiness when the expectations are not met, less obvious is the fact that expectations *equally* increase unhappiness when they *are* met. To understand why, we first have to identify the most important element in human happiness.

Expectations Undermine Gratitude, the Key to Happiness

Yes, there is a "secret to happiness"—and it is gratitude. All happy people are grateful, and ungrateful people *cannot* be happy. We tend to think that it is being unhappy that leads people to complain, but it is truer to say that it is complaining that leads to people becoming unhappy. Become grateful and you will become a much happier person.

Because gratitude is the key to happiness, anything that undermines gratitude must undermine happiness. And nothing undermines gratitude as much as expectations. There is an inverse relationship between expectations and gratitude: *The more expectations you have, the less gratitude you will have.* If you get what you expect, you will not be grateful for getting it. If you expect to wake up healthy tomorrow, and you do wake up healthy, you are most unlikely to be grateful for your health. On the other hand, if do you not expect to wake up healthy tomorrow, you will truly be grateful if you do. Most of us are grateful for anything we have only after we are threatened with losing it or actually do lose it—because then we no longer expect to have it.

Gratitude, the most important component of happiness, is largely dependent upon receiving what we do not expect to receive. That is why, for example, when we give children so much that they come to expect more and more, we actually deprive them of the ability to be happy—because they have less and less gratitude. This is why it is so important to teach children always to say "Thank you"—not only because it is the decent thing to do but because saying the words inculcates gratitude in the person saying them.

This is one of many reasons that religion, when done correctly, is important to happiness—it regularly inculcates gratitude. People who give thanks to God before each meal, for example, regularly inculcate gratitude in themselves. Can a secular family invoke gratitude at each meal? In theory, yes. The family members can bow their heads and thank the farmer who planted and harvested their food, the truckers who shipped it to market, and the local supermarket. But I have never heard of a family doing so.

Among Christians, for example, blessings of gratitude are regularly offered for food and at gatherings of friends. Having to express these words of gratitude on a regular basis undoubtedly induces some degree of gratitude. To cite another religious example of induced gratitude, Judaism even has a blessing over relieving one's body. This blessing, said to this day by many religious Jews upon leaving the bathroom, illustrates well the whole point of expectations and gratitude: "Blessed are You God, ruler of the world, Who created man in wisdom and created within him numerous orifices and spaces. It is known and revealed before You that if one of them should open when it should close or one of them should close when it should open, it would be impossible for us to exist. Blessed are You God, Who heals all mankind and does wonders." Very few people feel immense gratitude upon going to the bathroom, but people whose orifices opened when they should have closed or closed when they should have opened and who now relieve themselves normally do so with the kind of gratitude that the rest of us reserve for major events. For such people, and for those who express gratitude by reciting the bathroom prayer, trips to the bathroom induce gratitude and happiness.

Should We Have No Expectations at All?

How far should we take not having expectations? Should we have no expectations at all? Should I not expect to wake up healthy tomorrow? Should I not expect my airplane to arrive safely? Should children not expect their parents to love them?

Each of these questions will be answered. But first it is important to explain once again that *expectation* means taking for granted that something will happen or regarding something as virtually inevitable—as, for example, the sun rising tomorrow. Such certitude about the future is only possible in some areas of natural life, not in human life. Thus it is not my good fortune if the sun rises tomorrow, because the rotation of the earth is governed by immutable principles. But it is my good fortune if I and my loved ones wake up healthy tomorrow.

At the same time, abandoning expectations does not mean abandoning logic. If you ask me whether I assume, on the basis of the evidence, that I and my loved ones will wake up tomorrow without a grave illness, the answer is yes; I do not rationally believe that the chances are 50–50 that I will wake up tomorrow with cancer. But while I can take it for granted that the sun will rise tomorrow, I cannot take for granted a healthful tomorrow; one day I will not wake up healthy, but the sun will surely rise on that day.

Therefore, when I board an airplane, I would certainly bet, on the basis of statistics, that I will arrive at my destination safely. I would never have boarded if I thought otherwise. But a safe arrival, unlike the sun rising, is not inevitable, and so, while I would bet on a safe arrival, I do not absolutely expect it, and I am therefore grateful at every safe landing. I identify with those passengers from other cultures who applaud when their plane lands safely. They are expressing the gratitude that comes from not taking a safe landing for granted—and they are no doubt happier at their safe landing than those of us who express no such gratitude.

Thus, with rare exceptions, the answer to the question "Should we have no expectations at all?" is that *where we do not have full control,* we should not have expectations. And we do not have full control over most of the important things in life—our health and the health of those we love, how long we and those we love will live, or whether we will get a job we desire. We do, however, have control over some other important things. We control whether we expend our best effort; we control whether we act decently or not—we have moral free

61

will; and given health and ability, we also control the quality of our work.

With regard to having expectations of others, the same rule applies—we can have expectations of other people only in matters over which they have complete control—but with one additional emendation: we should have fewer expectations of others than of ourselves (for our sake and for theirs).

Children

One common example of other people of whom most of us have enormous expectations is children—expectations that are often injurious to both the parents and the children. We should have great *hopes* for our children, we should make certain *demands* of our children (e.g., that they not be mean to each other or to other children, that they do their homework), and we should help set *goals* for them. But we should keep our *expectations* of them quite limited. This is for their sake—they are autonomous human beings, not extensions of us; and for our sake—expectations of children often lead to gratuitous disappointment.

Spouses

Another example of people of whom we usually have expectations is spouses. These expectations too should be minimized. Of course, some basic moral expectations are valid and indeed necessary. For example, a wife can expect her husband not to beat her, and a husband can expect his wife not to run away with the children. But in general, the rules about expectations apply to marriage as to the rest of life. Indeed, expectations can easily hurt a marriage because the more we expect from our spouses, the more we are likely to take them for granted and the more we are likely not to feel grateful for all the good things they do. The combination of taking a spouse for granted and not feeling or expressing gratitude to them is fatal to most marriages.

One Exception—Children Should Expect Love

There is one major exception to not having expectations. Young children have every right to, indeed should, expect unconditional love from their parents. It is the birthright of every child to receive such love.

How Should We View the Future?

With greatly reduced expectations, how should we view the future? The answer is, we should have goals, hopes, and ambitions for ourselves; and we are right to make appropriate demands on others, such as fidelity from a spouse and honest work from an employee. But these are all different from expectations.

One should not assume for a moment that a lack of expectations means not being ambitious, not aspiring toward the highest goals, or not thinking positively. However, not having expectations does ensure two beautiful things: minimum suffering over unfulfilled goals and profound gratitude over goals that are fulfilled. There is little in life that gives so much at so little cost as not having expectations.

Objections to Reducing Expectations

Many people reject the goal of having fewer expectations, arguing that it is better to have expectations and to learn to cope with the hurt and disappointment they experience when those expectations are not fulfilled. To take the example of applying for a job, many people would argue that one should be able to say, "Though I really expected to get the job, I can cope with not having gotten it." I reject this view. While it is certainly true that if you have expectations, you cannot be happy unless you learn how to cope with grave disappointment when they are not fulfilled, there are no persuasive reasons to have expectations in the first place. The disadvantages of having expectations—lowered gratitude when they are fulfilled and gratuitous pain when they are not—greatly outweigh any advantages expectations may have.

One alleged advantage of having expectations is that it increases optimism. Not having expectations, it is argued, diminishes optimism, and optimism is essential to happiness. But not having expectations diminishes optimism *only* if we define optimism as the assumption that we will get what we want. Expecting to get what we want is immaturity, not optimism, and adults cannot long sustain happiness while holding immature beliefs.

Moreover, optimism has two dictionary definitions. One is the more immature one: "A tendency to expect the best possible outcome." The other is "To dwell on the most hopeful aspects of a situation." This definition of optimism is vitally necessary to happiness (see Chapter 23, "Find the Positive"), and it in no way conflicts with having diminished expectations. In fact, by greatly reducing our expectations, we greatly reduce the amount of disappointment in our lives, and reduced disappointment leads to *increased* optimism—because few people can retain optimism after suffering repeated disappointment.

In sum, those of us who have minimized our expectations walk around with a greater sense of thankfulness (because so many wonderful things that we didn't expect come our way each day) and with far less bitterness (because few, if any, expectations have been frustrated) than those who have expectations.

How do you begin minimizing expectations? First, do not fear that not having expectations will make you either less optimistic or less successful. Second, acknowledge the destructive role that expectations usually play in your life. Third, take an inventory of your life and begin to express gratitude for all the good in it. With each thing for which you regularly express gratitude, you will implicitly end your expectations of having it.

Chapter 14

Family

Little in life can bring us the happiness that we derive from our family. A parent's love for a child is perhaps the most powerful positive force in human life, and the love between a husband and wife is unique in the intimacy and depth of its bond. The family, for good reasons, has been the building block of all higher civilizations. And when good, it is also our refuge in a hostile world.

The operative words, however, are *when good,* for the family is not always good, and it can then present its members with serious obstacles to happiness.

The family is a classic example of the rule that whatever brings the most happiness can also bring the greatest unhappiness. Thus the family, which can provide so much love, security, and happiness to its members, is also the place that can create for its members a living hell, such as when children are physically, sexually, or psychologically abused by parents or other family members, are raised by an alcoholic parent, or are abandoned by a parent. The examples of intrafamily pain are virtually infinite.

But just as democracy is the worst form of government except for all the others, the family is the worst form of child rearing and male-female bonding except for all the others. It is not easy to do right. How could it be? Given the complexity of each family member and the exponential increase in complexity with the addition of every new family member, the rivalries of siblings, the tensions between parents, the disappointments, ambivalences, and miscommunications between parents and children, and the difficulties of each family member's own life, the wonder is not that many families function poorly but that so many families function as well as they do.

That an abusive family constitutes an obstacle to happiness is so self-evident, I will not discuss its being an obstacle to happiness. What is less self-evident and what is therefore important to discuss are the ways parents and children constitute obstacles to happiness even in nonabusive families.

Parents

Even completely loving parents are often obstacles to happiness. Again, how could they not be? It is easier to perform surgery than to raise happy, healthy, good children—and surgeons are given years of specialized training, while most of us have to raise human beings from babyhood to adulthood with nothing but our own parents' often very faulty model to guide us.

Parents are flawed human beings who are given a role that more approximates that of God than of mere mortals. No totalitarian tyrant has as much control over his subjects as even the kindest parents have over their young children. To a young child, the parent is a god. The parent is the source of everything a child needs—from physical nourishment and comfort to emotional nourishment and comfort. If the child's mother is in a bad mood, the child can feel virtually traumatized; if Dad is having troubles at work, the child can feel the weight of the world on his or her little shoulders.

The power of parents over children is almost unfair. And we, their children, live with the consequences of that power, whether faultily or properly used, forever. If our mother was too controlling or our father too remote, if our parents fought too much or didn't communicate enough, if either didn't show us enough love or enough understanding, if they didn't spend enough time with us or didn't respect us enough, or if they wanted us to compensate for their unhappiness in life, we can suffer from these pains for life.

For these reasons parents, our first loves who help make our happiness possible, are also, for many, genuine obstacles to happiness.

Because we cannot exchange our parents at a parents store (and even if we could, it would be at an age when much of their damage had already been done), there is no way for young children to avoid the unhappiness brought about by their parents. This is why other adults can and must help these children. Children respond to even the thinnest ray of love, just as plants respond to the thinnest ray of sun. Therefore we must love all the children who enter our lives, even if for brief periods. Adults who do not have children, grandparents, uncles and aunts, older cousins, friends of the family, teachers, clergy—virtually any adult not occupied all day with his or her own children—can play a critical role in the life of the great number of children who are not getting the proper amount and type of love from their parents.

The power of parents in our lives is such that even when we reach adulthood, the hurts of childhood can remain as obstacles to happiness—and continue as ongoing obstacles. For example, many adults who as young children did not receive sufficient love from their parents continue to yearn for that love, even when the parent is unable or unwilling to provide it. There comes a time when most of these adults must face the sad reality that a parent who has never been loving *will not change*. Yet many adults do not acknowledge this reality and go on hoping that they will one day receive the love they missed as children. Only when they can accept their inability to change their parent and perhaps even begin to enjoy the little intimacy in which this parent can engage will they begin to allow themselves to be happy. Unfortunately, this often happens only after many wasted years of frustration.

Not having received appropriate love from a parent is a real hole in a child's life. It is, to use the term I use in Chapter 9, a missing tile. But as I suggest in that chapter, when there is a missing tile in life, you must either find the tile or look elsewhere. If you cannot change your parent—and you usually cannot—look elsewhere for love. While nothing will precisely replace the missing love of a parent, life gives many of us a chance to fill the emotional holes of our childhood. You can greatly compensate for the missing love of your parent by loving your child. Becoming a loving parent gives many of us a second chance to have a home filled with love. You can also bask in the love of your husband or wife, in the love of friends, or in the love of relatives other than your parents. We need parental love, but that is not the only love available to us or the only love that can fill our heart.

Children

Nothing in my life has brought me greater joy than my children—raising them, learning from them, and loving and being loved by them. At the same time, we are denying reality if we deny that children are often an obstacle to happiness.

Someone ought to conduct a study comparing the happiness of married couples who have children with that of married couples who do not have children. No results would surprise me.

On the one hand, I wouldn't be surprised to learn that marriages with children were happier. For example, having children might allow many couples to accept a less happy marriage—children may be a compensation, as it were, for the less than wonderful relationship between the parents. Children can offer such couples a focus for their passions that the marriage may lack. And, of course, for happily married couples, children can offer the unique happiness that comes from raising and loving them.

On the other hand, I also wouldn't be surprised if studies concluded that in general children were more of an obstacle to marital happiness than a source of it. For most couples the arrival of a child is the first great challenge to their marital happiness.

Children are God's or nature's practical joke on couples—that which is produced by passion then proceeds to nearly kill it. The number of couples who have sexual relations—or take trips or have uninterrupted conversations—as frequently after having children as they did before is zero. Those who marry to have an intimate life companion—the best reason to marry someone—are in for the challenge of their life when children enter the scene. If parents are responsible, they will spend significant amounts of time with their child, and this is time that otherwise could be spent with each other. In many cases, too, one parent feels a competition with the child(ren) for the spouse's love and attention.

Moreover, these obstacles are created in the *best* of circumstances—when the child is healthy, has a kind disposition, has decent friends, does well in school, and is essentially happy. What if the child is often troubled, mean, chronically unhappy, seriously ill, hangs around bad peers, or fails in school? Then the challenge to the couple is far greater. Of course, a good marriage can withstand such challenges, but they *are* real challenges.

Many years ago, a dear friend, a bachelor, told me that one of the best things a troubled couple can do for their marriage is to have a child. I actually yelled at him. I needed to make the point as strongly as possible, lest when my friend marry one day he continue to believe such nonsense. Having a child is likely to make a troubled marriage worse (and being brought into a troubled home is certainly no favor to the child).

None of this is an argument against having children. I am only arguing that we must understand that children, while often a major source of happiness, are also an obstacle to it. Challenges and obstacles to happiness are not necessarily to be avoided, but they must be understood and confronted as such.

Siblings

Family challenges to happiness do not end with parents and children. The first glimmer most of us have of the obstacles we face in life comes from our siblings.

This must have dawned on people rather early in human history. The Book of Genesis is emphatic about intrafamily pain, especially sibling rivalry and even hatred. Genesis relates that the first brother in history is killed by his brother—Cain kills Abel. Jacob and Esau are paradigms of mutual hatred, and not only are they brothers, they are *twins*. And, of course, Joseph's ill treatment by and of his brothers is among the most famous stories in the Western world.

The day another child arrives home may be one of the happiest days in the lives of the parents, but to the new baby's siblings it is often one of the most miserable. That siblings can be, or can become, the closest of friends is certainly true, but it is far from being a given or even common. We fool ourselves when we say of close friends, "They are as close as brothers," because few brothers are as close as close friends. It would be far more accurate to say of close brothers, "They are as close as friends."

Parents must do all they can to foster affection among their children. Very few do. Most parents are so preoccupied with child-parent relationships that they devote little attention to their children's relationships with each other. It is not enough for parents to break up fights between siblings. Parents must also stop the teasing and other mean behavior between siblings. If their children are mean to other children, parents often scold their children, but if those children act in the same mean way to their siblings, parents frequently ignore it. This is hardly the way to foster sibling love, and many people therefore bear the scars of mean treatment by their siblings into adulthood.

Summary

How important an obstacle to happiness is the family? We can answer this by imagining how different the world would be if everyone were raised from birth by a happy, healthy, loving, attentive, and ethical mother and father (biological or adoptive). There would be far fewer police officers needed, far fewer wars fought, and far fewer books on happiness written. We wage battles within society, but the real battlefield for a better world, at least in a free society, is within the family.

Chapter 15

The World Has Too Much Pain

When people think about the challenge of being happy in the face of suffering, they usually think about their own lives—how to be happy in the face of their own suffering. But for many of us, there is another problem with regard to suffering—the suffering of others. Even if our own lives are relatively free of suffering, the suffering of others, including strangers, constitutes a serious obstacle to happiness.

Like most people, I have had to surmount serious problems and pain in my life. But I have always known that any pain I have experienced is minuscule in comparison to that of innumerable others—both people I know personally and, of course, people I have never met—and their suffering has been one of my greatest obstacles to happiness.

I am not unique in feeling this way. General human suffering must affect the happiness of any sensitive and decent person. The ubiquity of human suffering—particularly the suffering of the innocent at the hands of those who deliberately hurt them (as contrasted with suffering due to natural causes)—has unquestionably affected many people's happiness.* In fact, I often wonder if I am entitled to be as happy as I am, given the amount of suffering in the world.

I am therefore well aware of the challenge that human suffering poses to our happiness. Ultimately, however, I have chosen—it is a choice—not to allow human suffering to prevent me from being as happy as I can be. Here are my methods.

First, instead of allowing the world's evil to prevent me from being happy—which would only give evil another victory—I have chosen to fight it to the best of my abilities. I feel that this gives me "permission" to be happy. If I have made a difference in some people's lives by enabling them to enjoy some happiness, either through fighting against those who hurt them or by bringing them comfort, I feel free to be happy.

Second, happiness is important to doing good. Unhappy people are usually less capable than happy people of doing good. For one thing, they are usually too preoccupied with themselves and their unhappiness to do much good for others. For another, even if they want to do good for others, their unhappiness can easily cloud their judgment. And finally, when unhappy people try to help others by founding or joining social movements, they often do more harm than good. There are good reasons to fear social movements made up of unhappy people who want to bring about social change. Those left-wing and right-wing social movements that have destroyed tens of millions of lives were not composed of happy people. They were composed of unhappy people who blamed their unhappiness on others (for Nazis, Jews; for Communists, capitalists) and who looked to movements of radical social change as a source of both happiness and meaning. While there are times when the social order is so oppressive (living under a totalitarian regime is the best example) that personal happiness is essentially impossible, in relatively free

---

*Only *unjust* suffering presents us with emotional, intellectual, and moral problems. The *just* suffering of those who commit evil presents no such problem.

societies the sources of one's unhappiness are far more likely to be personal than social.

Third, instead of allowing the enormity of the world's suffering to make me unhappy, I have allowed it to increase the depth of my gratitude for the blessed life that I have been allowed to lead. You can look at the amount of suffering in the world and become bitter (this world stinks), cynical (nothing matters, it's all just a roulette game), or hedonistic (with all this suffering, I'll rack up all the fun I can)—or you can be grateful for your blessings.

Fourth, the ubiquity of unjust suffering made me realize long ago the intellectual and emotional necessity of a religious outlook on life. It seems to me that it would be extremely difficult for a truly secular person to be happy if he or she were sensitive to and fully aware of evil and suffering. The nonreligious view of the world holds that this unfair and often vicious life is the only reality (i.e., there is nothing beyond this life) and that whether one is blessed or cursed is essentially a matter of luck; whether one is tortured or blessed matters not at all to an uncaring universe. To believe this while caring deeply about those who are cursed with terrible misfortune would seem to make happiness nearly impossible.

The religious person who deeply cares about others does not necessarily have an explanation for any given individual's unfair suffering. Rather the religious person believes that a compassionate and just God rules the universe, and therefore there is meaning in all this apparent chaos.

This book is not the place to argue for the existence of God or the validity of religion. My only argument here is that belief in God and religion gives a person an intellectual basis for seeing the world as something other than a cosmos apathetic to the cries of children—thereby providing an important means of pursuing happiness in a world filled with pain.

Chapter 16

Seeking Unconditional Love

In 1995 the American Animal Hospital Association conducted a Pet Owner Survey, which found, among other things, that 57 percent of pet owners said that if stranded on an island, their preferred companion would be their pet, not a person.

This is not surprising. Increasing numbers of people look upon relationships with an animal companion (many animal lovers reject the term *pet*) as equal or even superior to relationships with people. Many Americans say that they love their pet more than they love almost any person. Over the course of twenty years, I have asked high school seniors throughout North America whether they would first save their dog or a stranger if both were drowning. In every instance (except for some religious schools), about one-third of the students vote to save the dog, one-third to save the human, and one-third simply cannot decide. When I ask the students who say they would first save their dog why they would do so, they answer, "I love my dog; I don't love the stranger." Even many adult callers to my radio show tell me that they prefer their dog (cat, hamster, rabbit, bird, monkey) to people because the animal is much more loving and loyal to them than any person.

I am convinced that a major reason for this growing preference for animals is that animals give unconditional love and people do not. And what could be more desirable than receiving unconditional love (i.e., being loved for doing nothing but existing)?

Yet seeking unconditional love is a vestige of childhood. Young children need, deserve, and therefore seek unconditional love. But *adults* should not need, do not deserve, and therefore should not seek unconditional love.

As adults, we should not need unconditional love. We should need the love of peers, which is not the same as the love we should have received as children from our parents. Moreover, unconditional love stymies growth into mature adulthood. If we will be loved no matter how we act, why should we act in a way that earns love?

At the present time, *earning love* is to many people a heretical concept. But acknowledging that when we are adults, love is in part earned is a cornerstone of maturing. Didn't I need to earn my wife's love when we dated? Why should I stop having to earn it now that we are married? To assume that no matter how I behave my wife will love me is to render me a child and her my mother. Undoubtedly many adults want to be children and want their spouse to be their parent, but this is far from healthy and therefore not a recipe for happiness.

Indeed, I suspect that those who receive unconditional love as children will not seek it as adults—because they have received what they needed when they needed it. Conversely, those who have been deprived of the love they should have been given as children will seek it throughout their lives (or at least until they work on themselves sufficiently to fully mature into adults).

Nor do adults deserve unconditional love. The idea that merely existing makes us deserving of others' love renders love infantile. While we deserve decent behavior from our fellow human beings, we have to earn their respect and love.

Because we neither need nor deserve unconditional love as adults, we should not seek it. If our parents did not give us unconditional love when we were young children, they will not start now. We cannot rely on unconditional love from our children once they have reached their teenage years. And our equals (i.e., friends and spouses) do not give it.

Thus seeking unconditional love is a guarantor of unhappiness, if only because we would be seeking something that no one will give us (except dogs). *Adult love is never unconditional.* As much as any husband and wife love each other, that love is not unconditional. There are—and should be—conditions under which a spouse's love can be lost. For example, no woman should continue to love a man who beats her.

What About God's Love?

Because human love for other humans (young children excepted) is not unconditional, many people have looked to God for unconditional love. This has profoundly helped many people live in an unloving world, especially if their earthly parents never gave them unconditional love.

For the record, however, my religious outlook does not posit a God who gives all people unconditional love. The source of my understanding of God, the Hebrew Bible, which originated the idea of a loving God, does not hold that whether we are the torturer or the torturer's victim, God loves us the same. Indeed, it implies that God's love is conditional (see, for example, Exodus 19:5, where God's love of His people is conditioned upon their keeping His covenant). I believe therefore that even with regard to God, we must try to grow into adulthood. God's love of us is immense and forgiving (if we repent) but not unconditional. In fact, I would have a difficult time loving a God who loved everyone equally. It would mean that God's love was unmoved by anything we do, and I cannot love that which cannot be moved.

Chapter 17

Seeing Yourself as a Victim

The Joy of Victimhood

There are some clear rules about happiness. One is that you cannot be happy if your primary identity is that of a victim, even if you really are one. There are a number of reasons:

- People who regard themselves as victims do not see themselves as in control of their lives. Whatever happens in their lives happens *to* them, not *by* them.

- People who primarily regard themselves as victims see the world as unfair to them in particular. Just as the young student who always sees himself as "being picked on" is an unhappy soul, so is the person who carries that attitude into adulthood.

- People who regard themselves primarily as victims are angry people, and an angry disposition renders happiness impossible.

- People who have chosen to regard themselves as victims cannot allow themselves to enjoy life, because enjoying life would challenge their perception of themselves as victims.

None of this is meant to deny that there are true victims. If you were rendered paralyzed by a drunk driver, you most certainly are a victim. The issue here is not whether there are real victims but the relationship of victimhood to happiness. Several years ago, my nephew Joshua Prager was traveling in a minibus that was hit by an out-of-control truck. At first rendered quadriplegic, he has improved almost miraculously to the point of only partial paralysis—he is now a reporter for the *Wall Street Journal*. While entirely realistic about the miserable twist of fate that ended his ball playing and trumpet playing, not to mention his ability to walk normally, he doesn't have a trace of victimhood thinking. This has enabled him to become one of the most life-loving and dynamic people I know.

In our time, however, the problem of regarding oneself primarily as a victim is not, ironically, so much a problem among actual victims such as my nephew as it is among people who have *decided* to see themselves as victims.

Such victims may be divided into five types: victims of their childhood, victims of membership in a group, victims of whatever makes them different, victims of perceived slights, and victims of deserved consequences.

The first group consists of individuals who walk around feeling victimized by their parents. In our psychological age, it is very tempting to see all unhappiness as emanating from psychopathological factors—and these are usually identified with one's upbringing. Just as people such as my nephew have been hurt by out-of-control drivers, there are people who have been hurt by out-of-control parents. These people merit our compassion, and they need help (including, but not exclusively, psychotherapy). But as much as the label *victim* applies to those hurt by their parent(s), to carry around a victim identity thoroughly undermines a person's ability to become happy.

Moreover, virtually all of us have in some ways been hurt by our parent(s). In terms of our upbringing, nearly all of us can consider ourselves victims. So common is it to inherit problems from parents that UCLA psychiatrist Dr. Stephen Marmer maintains that if we pass on to our children just half the neuroses we were given by our parents, we will have been exemplary parents!

Again, therefore, it is up to us to decide how long we choose to see ourselves as victims of our parent(s). Only on the day you begin to shed this identity can you begin to attain some happiness.

A second victimhood group consists of people who identify themselves as victims not necessarily because they have personally been victimized but because they are members of a group that has been victimized. Because almost every minority—and women as a group—has been victimized, a member of any of these groups can find it easy and tempting to assume a victim identity. Moreover, the *Zeitgeist* (spirit of the times) reinforces viewing entire groups as victims, and when society tells you that you should see yourself as a victim, it takes a particularly strong individual not to do so.

Thus many individuals have chosen to ascribe their personal unhappiness to their membership in a victimized group. Of course, in some cases, membership in a group does automatically render one a victim. Being a Jew in Nazi-occupied Europe, a black slave in the New World, an Armenian during World War I, a homosexual at various times in many countries, or a Cambodian during the Pol Pot era—just to cite a few of countless examples of terrible group suffering—meant that one was very much a victim. But today some people continue to view themselves as victims because of the *historical* suffering of their group and because it is easy and comforting to do so. And this renders happiness virtually impossible. First, as we have seen, perceiving yourself as a victim makes you unhappy. Second, it makes you permanently angry, which further guarantees unhappiness. Third, it enables you to avoid confronting whatever it is that is really making you unhappy.

A third form of victimhood thinking is blaming your unhappiness on whatever it is that makes you different. Some short men blame their height for much of their unhappiness. There are people who attribute their unhappiness to being adopted. I have even encountered a group of men who blame their unhappiness on having been circumcised. Examples are virtually endless.

The odds are overwhelming that unhappy short people, adoptees, and circumcised men would all be just as unhappy if they were not short or adopted or circumcised. This is easily proved: there are just as many unhappy people of normal height as there are unhappy short people, unhappy children of biological parents as of adoptive parents (indeed, the most comprehensive American study comparing adolescents adopted at birth with adolescents living with their biological parents found that those adopted were *better* adjusted),* and unhappy uncircumcised men as circumcised men (Jewish men, nearly all of whom are circumcised, are not a particularly unhappy group). Therefore, when people who are in any of these minorities begin to blame that fact for their unhappiness, they are doomed to greater unhappiness. One reason is that they are creating a problem where there really isn't one, and the other is that they are searching for the genesis of their unhappiness in the wrong place. They use whatever makes them different as a shield to prevent them from focusing on what truly ails them.

The fourth group consists of victims of perceived slights.

Once, at a dinner party, I learned that one of the guests, a fifty-year-old man I'll call Bob, had a twin brother. I asked him how they got along.

"We were very close until last year," he responded.

---

*The study, reported in the *New York Times*, June 23, 1994, was made by the Search Institute, a nonprofit, Minneapolis-based organization that conducts research on children and adolescents, and it was financed in part by the National Institute of Mental Health in Bethesda, Maryland. It found that:

"The adopted teenagers in the new study reported slightly fewer signs of high-risk behavior, such as binge drinking and theft, than did adolescents in the national sample."

"The adopted adolescents also scored better on 16 indicators of well-being, including friendships and academic achievement."

"Slightly more adopted adolescents, girls and boys, said they had a good sense of who they were and where they were going than did their nonadopted siblings."

"Of the adopted teenagers, 55 percent scored high on measurements of self-esteem compared with 45 percent of all teenagers in the institute's previous, larger study of adolescents nationwide."

These data do not apply to children adopted after the age of fifteen months.

"What happened?" I asked, quite amazed that two brothers could be close for forty-nine years and then suddenly drift apart.

His wife responded, "I threw Bob a fiftieth birthday party last year, and I didn't make the party for both brothers—though of course I invited Bob's brother and I even put his name on the cake."

As the story continued, I learned that Bob's brother could not get over the perceived insult of Bob's wife throwing a fiftieth birthday party for Bob and not for both of them. He felt this way despite the fact, Bob and his wife assured me, that the two brothers lived, worked, and socialized in different worlds and had no friends in common.

I listened in amazement, the insult seemed so trivial compared with the reaction. But of course this brother was not insulted by his brother and sister-in-law. It is, after all, quite understandable that grown men should have their own birthday parties. Rather, he had *decided to be insulted*. He *chose* to consider himself a victim of a perceived slight.

Another example was given to me by a woman at a card shop. She told me that when she checks bills of large denominations to determine if they are genuine or counterfeit, some customers get highly insulted—as if the test of their fifty-dollar bill somehow impugned their honesty.

Telling the difference between a real and a perceived insult may not always be easy, but it can and must be done. The reason we often err in perceiving a slight when none was meant is that we often *choose* to be hypersensitive—though only on our own behalf (just as when we err in money matters, we almost always err on our own behalf). We make this choice because of our insecurity, because of our anger at the other person, or because we want to play the role of victim. Whatever the reason, little is more destructive to happiness than perceiving yourself insulted when in fact you weren't.

If you find yourself feeling regularly insulted by people, try to seek out a fair outsider to help you determine whether your perceptions are accurate. If they are accurate, replace these people with people who will not insult you (or if you must keep some of these people in your life, fight back—you have no obligation to be demeaned). On the other hand, if your perceptions are not accurate, get rid of these perceptions—and find out why you have a predilection for perceiving slights when there are none.

The fifth group of victims is composed of those who have been victimized by their own behavior and then blame the deserved consequences of that behavior on others:

- The workers who are fired because of continuing irresponsible behavior and then blame their unemployment on the person who fired them

- The students who fail their exams and then blame their poor grades on their teachers

- The women who repeatedly fall for creepy men, ignore good men who are attracted to them, and then blame men for their social woes

These people are victims of their own behavior, and happiness will elude them until they come to realize this.

Why Victimhood Thinking Is Appealing

Given how destructive victimhood thinking is to happiness, one would think that people would do everything possible to avoid it. Unfortunately, this is not the case. Rather, it is yet another example of how we are usually the greatest obstacles to our own happiness.

Why do people choose victim status?

It Is Easier to Blame Others Than to Confront Life and Oneself

When we are unhappy, we are faced with a great choice: Do we recognize that life is inherently complex and filled with obstacles to happiness? Or do we blame others for our unhappiness? Of course, in some truly terrible instances—losing a loved one to a drunken driver, for example—it is quite valid to blame others for one's unhappiness. But when most unhappy people blame others, they do so because that is easier than to acknowledge life's complexity or to search within for the sources of their unhappiness.

Moreover, even when others do play a misery-inducing role in our lives, we still retain some control over our happiness. No matter how much outside forces may dominate our lives, there is one thing that we can virtually always control—how we react to them.

One book that deeply influenced me was *Man's Search for Meaning*, the memoir and observations of the psychoanalyst Viktor Frankl, who survived a Nazi concentration camp. One of his most important insights was that while the Nazis controlled everything in the inmates' lives, including whether they would live, starve, be tortured, or die, there was one thing the Nazis could not control—how the inmate reacted to all this.

That is the major reason I have found little relationship between the circumstances of people's lives and their level of happiness. If external circumstances determined people's happiness, happiness would be a simple rather than a complex subject. We would know whether people were happy simply by knowing their external circumstances, and we would never have to work on our happiness because we would never have any control over it. We could predict happiness according to two simple equations: Good Circumstances = Happy People; Bad Circumstances = Unhappy People.

The fact that such equations do not exist should convince anyone that blaming others or outside forces for our unhappiness is usually a mistake. Others can certainly contribute to our happiness or unhappiness, but it is we who make the final determination about how much we will allow others to affect our lives.

Victims Get Sympathy

Defining oneself as a victim is comforting for another reason—victims get, or think they will get, sympathy. Regarding oneself as a victim is therefore quite a powerful temptation. We get to blame others for our unhappiness *and* receive others' sympathy. What a great deal!

It Is Easier Not to Take Control of Your Life

Another factor that makes victimhood so tempting is that abandoning it means that we are responsible for making our own happiness. This is heady stuff. If you are used to being the master of your ship, it is empowering. But if you are not, it is frightening and therefore to be avoided. Personal responsibility is not an easy undertaking, and victimhood makes that undertaking unnecessary.

Self-Pity Is Addictive

We would do well to regard self-pity, which is an inevitable product of victimhood thinking, as an addictive drug. Experts on drugs contend that drugs are used, first and foremost, to medicate pain. Self-pity serves a similar function, and as with narcotics it becomes increasingly difficult to stop relying on it. Furthermore, as with addiction to drugs, addiction to self-pity can render a person destructive to self and others—destructive to the self because it is easy to wallow in self-pity and allow it to paralyze action; destructive to others because the more that people consider themselves victims, the angrier they will be and the likelier they are to lash out at others.

It Is Hard to Mature

The ultimate reason people take on a victim mentality is immaturity. It takes maturity to avoid tempting but destructive choices; it takes maturity to want to be in control of your life and not to be controlled; and it takes maturity not to allow yourself in times of crisis to wallow in self-pity.

The problem in our time is that maturity is not high on the list of goals we offer the next generation. We stress happiness, success, and intelligence but not maturity. And that is too bad, both for society, which suffers when too many of its members are immature, and for the individual who wants to be happy. For happiness is not available to the immature. And one of the prominent characteristics of immaturity is seeing oneself primarily as a victim.

Chapter 18

The Opposite Sex

For most people, a loving relationship with someone of the opposite sex is an incomparable source of happiness. All its challenges notwithstanding, the marriage of a man and a woman can be the greatest antidote to loneliness and the greatest source of emotional growth and happiness.

Nevertheless, just as the family can be both a source of happiness and an obstacle to it, the same is true of the opposite sex. Men and women are so different from each other that the wonder is not that so many do not get along but that so many do. This is one reason marriage can be such a great source of personal growth—learning how to get along well with someone so different from ourself is a great achievement. There are surely times when men and women see their differences as so great that they are convinced the opposite sex is not merely another sex but another species.

The challenge to happiness lies in the fact that not only are men and women different from each other, but these differences bring conflict as well as comfort. We therefore now turn our attention to one of the differences that can cause major conflict between men and women.

Men, Women, and Their Different Areas of Insatiability

As noted in the chapter on human nature, our nature is insatiable. This is equally a problem for men and women. However, men and women are also insatiable in *distinct* ways, and these ways frequently cause tension between the two sexes.

In general, both sexes have equally insatiable natures, and they often share areas of insatiability. For example, men and women can be equally afflicted with an insatiable drive for material possessions. While this can be a serious obstacle to their ever being content, it does not necessarily cause serious tension between two individuals. But the insatiable drives that are distinct to each sex can, and often do, cause disharmony between the sexes. Recognizing these areas of incompatible insatiability can therefore be very helpful in fostering male-female harmony.

Among men, this area of insatiability is sexual variety; and among women, it is emotional intimacy.

I realize that this understanding of male and female nature runs counter to some present-day thinking and that it can be painful to read, but if we are truly interested in confronting human nature as a source of unhappiness and in overcoming it, we must describe human nature as honestly as we can.

Male nature is designed not to feel content sexually but rather to lust for yet another partner (as distinct from lusting for more sex with the same partner, a desire that can characterize both sexes). This desire for more sexual partners is not socially induced but a part of male nature. One proof is that it is as true for homosexual men as it is for heterosexual men. Another proof is the multibillion-dollar pornography industry. It is almost entirely male oriented—again, whether heterosexual or homosexual—and it offers an endless supply of new lust objects. If male nature were not variety oriented, one issue of *Playboy* would suffice forever.

Moreover, the yearning for different sexual partners is true for men who have frequent sex and for men who have little sex, for bachelors and for married men, for men who love their partners and for men who are unhappily married. In other words, it is true for nearly all men. For most men, it is *monogamy,* not the search for different sexual partners, that is the result of social influence.

Lest any of this description of male sexual nature be misinterpreted, I need to make it clear that it is offered only to describe an area of insatiability that can be a source of unhappiness to men and their wives; it is in no way a defense of men who act upon their insatiable nature.

Understandably, this aspect of men's nature is painful to many women, especially when they first learn of it. Yet truth to tell, it is not only painful to women; it is painful to all men who wish to live life on a higher plane than male mammals. And unlike women, who can ignore this painful facet of male nature (although they should not do so), men can never ignore it; it is an omnipresent burden.

But women also have their burden.

Lest there be a terrible imbalance of insatiability between the sexes, God or nature gave women a correspondingly insatiable urge and wisely ensured that it be an urge that works in the opposite direction of the male urge. If women equally possessed the male drive for numerous partners, the world would self-destruct: few people would marry and make a family, nothing lasting would be built, men and women would devote their lives to lust satiation, unattractive men and women would be ignored, and the human race would differ little from the animal kingdom.

What was necessary to counterbalance men's powerful drive toward sexual variety was an equally powerful female drive toward emotional intimacy, a desire that is in many ways a mirror image of man's desire for variety. Just as a man's sexual yearning for yet another body cannot be fully satisfied, a woman's yearning for intimacy is rarely fully satisfied. Just as it is difficult to imagine a man announcing, "I am so sexually satisfied with one woman that I have no sexual desire for other women," it is hard to imagine a woman saying, "I am so satisfied with the amount of emotional intimacy in my life that I wish no deeper level of intimacy and no more intimate time with anyone in my life, whether my husband, my mother, my children, or anyone else."

A major source of marital discord in good marriages, not to mention bad ones, emanates from the woman's yearning for more intimacy and the man's lack of such yearning and/or from his yearning for more sex with her or with others.

For all the tensions that result from the differences between male and female natures, neither sex would really want things to be much different. Let men imagine what women would be like if they had men's nonintimate, variety-directed, always-seeking-new-excitement nature. Men would loathe such competitive women, few people would establish a stable home (which despite their nomadic nature, most men yearn for), and few men or women would take care of the next generation. On the other hand, let women imagine what men would be like if they were as desirous of intimacy, as nest-oriented, as women. Most women regard men who are like that as essentially women with men's bodies, not as desirable men. It is the rougher edged, macrooriented, and sexually aggressive male nature that makes men—*when they control their nature*—most attractive to women.

In other words, women want men to be men, and men want women to be women. But manly men and womanly women come with a price—their distinct nature.

What to Do

There are ways of ameliorating this problem. First, men and women must acknowledge that the sexes have different natures and different areas of insatiability.

We begin this process by understanding our own sex. The moment we can recognize that our male or female nature has elements of insatiability, we are in a much better position to deal with the frustration involved in not satisfying our drive. The greatest frustrations in life take place when we believe that something unattainable can be attained. Thus a presidential candidate who fails to become president is frustrated, but most of us are not frustrated at not becoming president, because we do not consider the presidency attainable.

If a man thinks that sexual contentment is attainable (e.g., by sleeping with yet another partner), he is setting himself up for immense frustration and unhappiness. His powerful drive is fooling him, and he needs to use his mind to counteract his nature.

Let us suppose that he does manage to sleep with a new woman. What happens the next day, week, or month? He is back where he was the day before he had his affair—lusting for someone new (except that he now has potentially disastrous marital and other problems). For most men, to attain ongoing sexual contentment would involve a king's lifestyle of an endless supply of attractive women. And even then, sexual contentment is not guaranteed, since all thrills diminish in time.

This realization is also one of the most effective arguments against a man having an extramarital affair. If man's sexual nature were such that a new partner once a year, let us say, actually gave him a year's worth of sexual peace, an argument for an extramarital affair on purely sexual (i.e., nonmoral) grounds could be made. But a sexual affair doesn't quell a man's urge for variety for anything approaching a year. Shortly after his affair, he is back to sexual square one.

None of this argues against the importance of a good sex life for a husband (or a wife). That a man's sexual urge for variety cannot be fully satisfied does not mean that there are not better and worse sex lives. Although sexual relations constitute a tiny fraction of a marriage in terms of time, it is a tiny fraction that can make or break the rest of the marriage. A good (good, not fully satisfying) sex life is therefore important to a good marriage.

But the man must know that even in the best circumstances—frequent and satisfying sexual relations with a partner whom he loves—he will still walk around (especially in contemporary Western societies, with their sexual bombardments) with sexual frustration. He must continually remind himself of the insatiability of his sexual nature and (when possible) come to appreciate the sex life that he does have.

At the same time, the woman must continually grapple with the fact that she can never fully satisfy her emotional nature. Even in the best of circumstances—marriage to a loving husband who is intimate and communicates well—she will still have her frustrations. She will still want more time with her beloved, more intimacy—and if not more of her husband, then more of her children, her mother or father, a sibling, a friend. For a woman to know this about her nature can be very liberating. By knowing about her insatiable nature, she can come to appreciate (when possible) the intimacy that she does have.

And just as a woman must do what she can to help her man with his sexual nature (first and foremost by attempting to understand it), a man must do whatever he can to help his woman with her nature (first and foremost by attempting to understand it) and establish a deeper and more intimate relationship with her—more time alone, more gestures like flowers for no particular reason, and more hugging and tenderness.

There is one other way to describe this problem: *desires have no memory, only the mind does.* If a man sees a sexy woman in a bikini a day after having wonderful sex with his beloved, he may desire that woman as if he hadn't had sex in a month. His urge has no memory; and his mind must remind him of that. Likewise, if a woman has a wonderfully intimate vacation alone with her man, upon their return home and his return to his normal work schedule her desire for intimacy may make her think they are never intimate. Her desire has no memory; and her mind must remind her of that.

Attaining happiness means doing constant battle with our nature. To do that we must first know what our nature is, and then we must control it. It is never easy. In the case of the sexes it is particularly difficult.

Chapter 19

Genes or Biochemistry

When they are born, some children, if they could speak, would say, "Thank you. Thank you so much for bringing me into this beautiful world. I am thrilled and grateful to be here."

Other children, if they could speak, would say something different: "I never asked to be conceived. I never asked to be removed from the warm, secure place you just took me from. Because you did, I will make your life miserable." These children seem to start out life unhappy.

As any parent can confirm—and studies increasingly show—we are born with certain personality traits. Whether these are entirely genetic, formed partially in utero, the characteristics of our unique soul, or a combination of all three is the subject of other books. What is crucial in our context is to note that some of us are born with a personality predisposed toward happiness and some with a personality predisposed toward unhappiness; some of us have moody personas, and some of us have generally cheerful ones.*

Biochemical Origins of Unhappiness

Before confronting this often unfortunate fact, one other "built-in" predilection toward unhappiness needs to be acknowledged. Not everyone who is chronically unhappy was born that way; many of these people became unhappy at some time in life, perhaps as early as infancy (and therefore think they were born that way). And among these people, their chronic unhappiness either came from, or brought about, a biochemical change that resulted in some form of depression.

Thus while most unhappiness is a function of circumstances, attitude, and/or psychology, some unhappiness has biochemical origins (and this biochemistry may well have been brought about by traumatic circumstances).

Biochemically induced unhappiness cannot be undone by attitudinal, circumstantial, and therapeutic changes alone. Biological roots of unhappiness may necessitate biological solutions. This means that some people's chronic unhappiness may be clinical depression that must be treated in part by a psychopharmaceutical drug such as Prozac. The argument that such drugs are overprescribed is true but irrelevant. Antibiotics are overprescribed, but no one denies that they are sometimes necessary.

---

*One puzzle whose solution lies beyond the scope of this book is why these two types almost always marry each other. In all my life, I have never met a moody married to a moody—which proves that the moody may be unhappy, but they are not dumb. This does not mean that the nonmoody are always dumb for intermarrying—the nonmoody often need a moodier partner for emotional balance. Furthermore, many people hide their unhappy disposition while dating, which is relevant to our purposes because it shows that a great number of people can, when the rewards are great enough, act happier than they feel.

Three Misconceptions About Psychiatric Drugs

Three common misconceptions about drugs such as Prozac need to be addressed. The first is that those who take these drugs never confront the real sources of pain in their lives. The second is that psychiatric drugs "make" people happy and that therefore when these drugs work, people's newly acquired happiness is artificial. The third is that there is some shame in having to rely on a psychiatric drug—that people should be able to solve their problems without drugs.

Regarding the first objection, people who take a psychiatric drug but who do not confront their psychological impediments to happiness will simply not heal. A drug treating biochemical problems obviously treats only biochemical origins of depression. On the other hand, once biochemical healing begins, people should be able and inspired—since the fog is finally beginning to lift—to confront the psychological origins of their depression (which may be the ultimate cause of the biochemical imbalance).

The second misconception about psychiatric drugs is that they induce artificial happiness. This is a misconception because psychiatric drugs do not *make* anyone happy; they only *enable* people to *become* happy. Drugs such as Prozac no more make a person happy than a cast on a broken leg makes a person a track star. The leg cast enables the leg to heal so that a person may eventually be able to run again. How fast the person runs will depend on personal effort, health, innate abilities, and so on. Prozac enables the body to heal so that a person may be happy—how happy depends upon personal effort, psychological health, innate disposition, circumstances, and so on. That is why it is invalid to maintain that any happiness achieved by people who take a Prozac type of drug is artificial. One might as well say that the track victories of a runner who had leg surgery were artificial.

The third misconception is that there is some sort of shame in taking psychiatric drugs. The feeling is that either such people don't have the fortitude to confront their real problems and have instead resorted to the easy way out or that they are so sick that they need drugs. It is quite remarkable that at the end of the twentieth century there are otherwise sophisticated people who hold such views. They can only be explained by ignorance and prejudice. The ignorance is of the effect of biology on happiness, and the prejudice is the age-old one against believing that mental illness is ever analogous to physical illness.

My heart goes out to anyone who can be helped by a psychiatric drug but refuses to take one because of any of these misconceptions. And my anger is directed toward those who argue against all psychiatric drugs. There is, for example, an American physician, a psychiatrist no less, who runs an institute dedicated to persuading people never to take psychiatric drugs. One of his arguments is that women who suffer from depression do so because of sexism in society, never because of biochemistry. I have never heard how this doctor explains male depression. Perhaps it is due to capitalism.

All these arguments notwithstanding, I do believe that taking a psychiatric drug must always be a *last resort*. It should only be used after therapy, religion, and other efforts have been made and failed to stem the depression. In addition to those efforts, the individual should also consider changing his or her diet and even taking vitamins under the guidance of nutritional and medical experts. The effects of diet on our mood are remarkable. Furthermore, patients taking a psychiatric drug should aim, when feasible, to wean themselves off the drug eventually.

I would not have devoted years to speaking and writing on happiness if I believed that most unhappiness is biologically based. Every other chapter of this book is premised on the belief that unhappiness can be reduced by changes in one's attitudes and philosophy of life. Nevertheless, as much as any of us might wish that all unhappiness be societally, psychologically, or philosophically treatable, some just is not.

Some of us are either born with a biological predisposition toward unhappiness or depression or acquire such a predisposition at some point, usually at a young age. It is important that we know this about ourselves, and it is important that we know this about a loved one.

If we are the ones with such a predisposition, we might be able to treat it and, just as important, accept it. If we are, in fact, "built" this way, we no longer have to blame ourselves or loved ones for our unhappiness. There is something worse than depression—blaming it on yourself or a loved one.

If it is a loved one who is predisposed to unhappiness, we can finally face the liberating reality of not feeling responsible for making that person happy. The large number of children who feel responsible for their parents' unhappiness, of parents who feel responsible for their children's unhappiness, and of husbands and wives who feel responsible for their spouse's unhappiness, all produce a sea of tears in each generation. If you or a loved one is continually depressed, the chances are that no loved one can make a difference. You must see a psychiatrist and end the cycle of blame.

Part III

Attitudes and Behaviors That Are Essential to Happiness

Chapter 20

Meaning and Purpose

Happiness can be attained under virtually any circumstances providing you believe that your life has meaning and purpose. It was the psychoanalyst Viktor Frankl, in *Man's Search for Meaning,* who first made me aware of the incomparable significance of meaning to happiness. It was as a prisoner in a Nazi death camp that Frankl observed in the starkest possible way that people need a sense of purpose to maintain a will to live.

The need for meaning and purpose is not only of monumental importance to happiness, it is one of the primary distinguishing characteristics of the human being. Some animals may have emotions and the ability to communicate with each other and even with humans. However, at least one difference is unbridgeable—animals do not need to have meaning in their lives. Human beings, on the other hand, crave meaning. In Viktor Frankl's view, the human need for meaning is as great as and perhaps greater than any other need. For example, as powerful as the sex drive is, there are people who have been able to lead happy lives without engaging in sexual relations. But it is most unlikely that anyone who lacked a sense of purpose and meaning has ever led a happy life.

Even the fundamental human need to be with other people may

not be as great as the human need for meaning. In his memoirs of his days as a Soviet dissident, Anatoly (Natan) Sharansky wrote that even when he suffered the torment of solitary confinement, he was a happier person than his guards because his life, unlike theirs, had meaning and a sense of purpose.

The Types of Meaning

Most contemporary discussions about meaning in life focus on the importance of people finding meaning in their lives. But finding meaning in our lives is not enough for the attainment of deep happiness. People derive meaning from two beliefs—the belief that *their* life has meaning and the belief that *life itself* has meaning. Both beliefs—in personal meaning and in transcendent meaning—are necessary for happiness.

There are people who have neither belief, people who have both beliefs, and increasingly there are people who have only one of these beliefs—that their own lives have meaning, while life itself is ultimately meaningless. Among the latter are many secular intellectuals, who see human life as a random, undirected coincidence yet (essentially for the sake of their sanity) continue to regard their personal lives as meaningful. On purely logical grounds, I do not see how a meaningless universe can produce meaningful lives, but I well understand why most people who believe in a meaningless universe do not wish to view their own lives in this way.

Personal Meaning

For nearly all of us, personal meaning is derived from three sources—relationships (family and friends), work, and causes.

Relationships   Most people, especially parents, know well how much personal meaning can be derived from family life. For example, few things in life are as meaningful as raising a child. A parent is the primary physical, emotional, psychological, moral, and financial support of a child. Such a role provides a person with as much personal meaning as anything can. And from the perspective of the emotions, few things give us as much meaning as the smiles of children, their opening up to us, and their blossoming into adulthood under our care.

Nor do you have to be a parent to appreciate the meaningfulness of family. We derive immense meaning from loving, being loved, belonging, and being needed—and all of these are obtainable in family life. In addition, most men derive meaning from providing materially for their family, and most women derive meaning from providing emotional sustenance for their family (of course, both sexes can and increasingly do provide both material and emotional sustenance). Meanwhile, young children derive almost all their meaning from their membership in a family.

Friends provide meaning in much the same way. In fact, children who do not have friends, even if they have a good family life, are at greater risk for later depression and other emotional and social problems. And one of the most difficult features of growing old is the loss of friends.

Work A second major source of personal meaning for many people is work, and such meaning is unrelated to its monetary compensation. Lawyers may have a huge annual income, for example, yet their work may provide little meaning if it involves defending people or organizations for whom they have little respect. On the other hand, many people who earn much less, such as teachers, or who earn nothing, such as volunteers, find their work to be profoundly meaningful.

Because many people look to work for money or prestige more than for meaning, work is not particularly meaningful for them and therefore not much of a source of happiness. One obvious lesson, then, is that we often have to choose between income and meaning in the work we do.

A Cause The third common source of personal meaning is attachment to a cause. Of the three sources of personal meaning cited here, attachment to a cause can be the most powerful, but it is also the most perilous: its power for evil is as great as its power for good. When the causes are, for example, conquering disease or protecting children, the cause is both meaningful and good. Some causes, however, can be meaningful but not good.

This can happen when people attach themselves to a cause because they lack any other source of personal meaning. Then the cause becomes a substitute for other meaning-givers, especially human relationships. This is one reason young single people more readily give their lives over to causes than do married adults. Since they have no spouse or children, rarely have the deep friendships that come with age, and are unlikely to have life-fulfilling work, a cause becomes their greatest source of meaning and therefore of happiness (and even of relationships—with other members of the cause).

Of course, when attachment to a cause is the source of meaning in a person's life, and the cause is a truly noble one, the world may well benefit from this commitment. But if the person's attachment to a cause is the result of a search for meaning that is otherwise absent, the cause can easily be less than noble and may even be cultlike. History is filled with examples of people who have looked to causes for meaning and done great evil through them. This is especially true of men because they do not naturally find relationships as fulfilling as most women do (men can learn, however).

The cause that has given more men and women meaning and happiness than any other is religion. Given that other characteristics of religion—community and transcendence—also provide happiness, it is not surprising that religion can be the most powerful force for both good and evil. Indeed, the record of religion is mixed. Most major religions have done more good than harm, but some have done a great deal of harm.

Nevertheless, the weakening of religion as a source of meaning for individuals in the modern era has been considerably more of a curse than a blessing. With the decline of traditional religion, tens of millions of people have looked elsewhere for causes to provide meaning, and the most popular of these have created enormous evil—ideologies such as chauvinistic nationalism, racism, Communism, and

Nazism. While some individuals have attached themselves to causes outside of religion that have been moral, the moral record of people in the twentieth century who have given their lives over to large-scale social causes outside of religion has usually been awful.

In sum, causes are great meaning-givers, but they are best for the world when the people who attach themselves to those causes derive essential meaning in their lives from human relationships, not from the cause itself. The biographies of human monsters like Adolf Hitler and Josef Stalin, of evil cult leaders, and of America's serial murderers are virtually all biographies of loners.

Transcendent Meaning

Most thinking people understand how important it is to find personal meaning in their lives. But personal meaning is not enough; to be happy, thoughtful people must also believe that life itself is meaningful.

This is where the modern secular world often undermines people's happiness. A purely secular understanding of existence can only mean that the world ultimately has neither purpose nor meaning. This is not the place to argue which view of the universe—the religious understanding of a purposeful universe or the secular understanding of a random one—is more accurate. There is, after all, no way to know. What is knowable is the consequences of the two views.

If there is no God, no Higher Being, no ultimate guiding hand that imbues creation with meaning and purpose, then creation does not have those qualities. As much as we may find our work, family, friends, and social causes a source of meaning, a secular universe means that there is no ultimate meaning to any of these things. We have *made up* all these meanings in order not to despair. It is quite difficult to be happy if we stare into the mirror each morning and see only the random product of meaningless forces, stellar dust that happens to be self-aware.

This is why a religious perception of the universe is so important to the happiness of people who think about life. While the dominant intellectual view of our time posits that the less thoughtful individuals are those who most need religion, in fact *it is the thinker who most needs religion*. For, at least in theory, the nonthinker can be happy solely by experiencing life's pleasures and personal meaning, but the thinker knows that pleasures and personal meaning alone do not answer the human yearning for a meaningful universe.

Conclusion: Always Ask, "Is It Meaningful?"

To be a good person, it is always necessary to ask before doing something, "Is it right?" To be physically fit, it is necessary to ask before eating something, "Is it healthful?" To be a happy person, it is necessary to ask before acting, "Is it meaningful?" The problem, of course, is that the good action, the healthful food, and the meaningful behavior are rarely the most enticing of our choices—which only proves, once again, that the greatest battle for happiness is with our own nature.

Chapter 21

Happiness
Is a By-product

As important as happiness is, if you make it your most important value, you cannot attain it. Happiness is only achievable when it is a by-product of something else, and you must hold that something to be more important than happiness.* Moreover, it is impossible to fool yourself. You cannot, for example, say, "In order to be happy I will value x more than happiness," while in your heart continuing to value happiness more.

I offer six values that are widely held to be more important than happiness—and that therefore bring people much of it.

---

*Ask parents today what they most want for their children, and the vast majority of them will tell you that they want their children to be happy. As well intentioned as this is, by making happiness the greatest value in their children's lives, these parents are, unfortunately, making it far harder for their children to be happy adults. Parents who want their children to be happy but who raise them to believe that some values are even higher than happiness are more likely to raise happy children.

Passionate and Meaningful Pursuits

The first and perhaps most obvious sources of happiness are those pursuits for which people feel great passion and that give people's lives meaning. The number of such pursuits is almost infinite—from studying insects to a career in baseball to comforting the dying.

Because of the power of passionate and meaningful pursuits to bring us happiness, it is essential to help children develop as many passions as possible. The more passions we have—whether for people, things, work, hobbies, or something else—the greater happiness we are likely to experience. But again, we cannot fool ourselves. Having a passion for something is not enough. It must have intrinsic value and meaning. Thus a person may have a passion for watching television, but watching television in great amounts is neither intrinsically valuable nor meaningful, and it is therefore not conducive to happiness.

I rarely cite studies, believing that they usually either find what common sense and human experience already know or whatever the study-maker wanted to find, but regarding the relationship between happiness and television watching, I have seen studies that have opened my eyes. These studies found that after a certain amount of television watching on any given day, people actually become less happy. Now one might counter that after a certain amount of time doing any one thing, one will become less happy. But this is not true. Take, for example, something as esoteric and uninteresting to most of us as studying insects. Because such study, unlike television watching, can be both intrinsically valuable and meaningful, a person who loves studying insect life will not become more unhappy after a certain amount of time studying insects. Six hours a day (the average amount of time spent watching television in an American home) devoted to studying insects can actually increase the happiness of a person—because it leads to growth and knowledge.

To cite another example, although a *career* in sports can bring a person happiness—thanks to the person's love of the sport, deep interaction with others in the game, and the mental, physical, and emotional challenges of the sport—merely being a sports fan (i.e., *watching* sports) after a certain amount of hours does not bring a person happiness. Watching sports is a source of *fun* but rarely a source of meaning to fans. One proof is the vast amount of gambling on sports among fans. Gambling gives watching sports a meaning that it otherwise lacks. On the other hand, watching sports can be meaningful to those involved in management, player development, and sports writing.

Depth

A second example of a goal that yields happiness as a by-product is depth. At the present time, depth (along with maturity) is almost never cited or even considered when people—especially young people—think about what they wish to achieve. Ask most people, "How important is being deep to you?" and you are likely to receive a puzzled response: "What do you mean?"

The subject of becoming a deeper person deserves its own book, so I will offer only a brief definition and a few examples. Perhaps the best way to understand depth is to think of growth: we become deeper when we *struggle to grow*—emotionally, morally, psychologically, intellectually, and in wisdom. Note, please, that struggle is part of depth. Very little that is acquired easily is deep.

However, human nature once again works against us. Human nature motivates us to seek immediate pleasure, not depth. Yet those who transcend their nature and seek depth will derive great happiness from that struggle.

Who is likely to be intellectually deeper (and happier)—the person who devotes most evenings to reading good books, taking courses, and studying a foreign language or a musical instrument or the one who devotes most evenings to watching television?

Who is likely to be emotionally deeper—the person who commits to a relationship, marries, and raises children or the single person who goes from relationship to relationship?

Who is likely to be psychologically deeper—the person who

devotes time and effort to learning about herself/himself or the one who rarely looks within?

Examples apply to every area of life. Even fun can be deepened. You can relax with hours of card playing or by involving yourself with interests that make demands on you, such as taking an adult education course. You can enjoy "easy listening" music, or you can make the effort to enjoy deeper music such as classical music. You can watch movies that just entertain or watch movies that provoke thought as well as entertain. You can read pop novels that just entertain or read novels that make intellectual and emotional demands as well as entertain.

When you have experienced deeper fun, it is difficult to go back to the more superficial variety because the rewards of depth are great. Ask anyone who has truly enjoyed both popular and classical music which one ultimately brings greater rewards (and I say this with a deep appreciation of the joys of popular music).

Pursuing depth is one of the distinguishing characteristics of the human being; it is one of the noblest goals of a human life; and it brings ongoing happiness. Indeed, the journey to depth brings as much happiness as its attainment, and since depth has no limits, the journey to it never ends.

Wisdom

A third goal whose pursuit brings happiness as a by-product is wisdom. Wisdom may be defined as *understanding*, as opposed to merely *knowing*. Knowledge is wonderful, but it is not the same as, not as valuable as, and does not bring the happiness or peace of mind that wisdom brings. Computers have a great deal of knowledge, but they have no wisdom. Indeed, this is true of many humans. If accumulating knowledge inevitably brought one wisdom, given the number of well-educated people today, we would be living in the wisest age in humanity's history; and given how few people in the past received much education, few of our ancestors could have been wise.

Yet probably all of us have known someone of limited education who possessed great wisdom, and all of us know some highly educated people who are quite foolish.

I offer no sure path to wisdom; there probably is none. Some people seem to be born with wisdom, and some attain it through great intellectual and emotional struggle. What is clear is that a lifelong pursuit of wisdom yields a happier life.*

Clarity—Understanding Yourself and Life

A fourth goal higher than happiness that produces happiness as a by-product is clarity. We might be tempted to think that we can be happy without working to understand ourselves and life—believing in a form of "ignorance is bliss"—but this is not so. From traditional Eastern thought to modern Western psychological thought, there is widespread acknowledgment that clarity, even when painful, is a blessing, not a curse. Great numbers of people walk through life with little understanding of why life behaves the way it does or why they themselves behave the way they do. Yet to understand why your life unfolds in the way it does is one of the greatest sources of happiness.

One reason is that we are far more capable of handling life's

---

*For the interested reader, I offer two theories to explain, in large part, the decline in wisdom in our time. One is specialization in education: a broad-based education has been abandoned in favor of accumulating an immense body of knowledge in increasingly narrow areas of specialization. The other is the assertion in Proverbs that "Wisdom begins with awe of God." Secularization has led to a number of blessings, most notably the blessing of tolerance, thanks to secular government. But it rarely leads to wisdom. How could it? The denial of any transcendent meaning to human life leads ultimately to the belief that all is random and rather pointless. And there is little wisdom to be culled from randomness and meaninglessness. We correctly associate most religious government with a lack of tolerance. We should just as correctly associate most secular thought with a lack of wisdom.

tragedies when we have some explanation for them. For example, when an airplane accident is explained, the friends and relatives of the passengers who died are in a better emotional position than the friends and relatives of the victims of a crash that has no explanation. If clarity and understanding were not immensely important to our happiness, explaining such accidents would not matter. Yet having explanations (i.e., having clarity) matters a great deal. A lack of clarity suggests that our life is in chaos; chaos suggests meaninglessness; and meaninglessness guarantees unhappiness.

As with all growth and depth, the more you understand, the more you want to understand. You will want to know why you lost your temper, why you yelled at a loved one, why you keep falling in love with the wrong type of person. Clarity cannot change everything that will happen in our life, and it will certainly not change anything that has happened, but it transforms us from passive bystanders to actors.

Goodness

A fifth example is elevating doing good over being happy. I write elsewhere of the connection between goodness and happiness—for example, good people bring other good people into their lives, and spending our lives with such people increases our happiness. People who make doing good and attaining good character more important goals than achieving happiness achieve happiness as a by-product of that goal. The peace of mind and sense of self-worth that derive from the pursuit of goodness are unattainable elsewhere.

Pursuit of the Transcendent

The final example is perhaps the most ubiquitous—pursuit of the transcendent. Throughout history, most people have been acutely aware of the ephemeral nature of human life. We arrive against our will, stay a short while, and leave against our will. Today we also know that we are infinitesimally small specks in the vast universe. Consequently, more than ever we need meaning that can come only from the belief that something permanent transcends us.

Many will argue that there is no transcendence and that religion is largely nonsense, even dangerous nonsense. But few can argue against the proposition that religion is capable of bringing more inner peace than anything else. There is something in the human being that yearns for the meaning, order, community, and answers that religion uniquely provides.

Chapter 22

Develop Perspective: Cultivate a Philosophy of Life

We Determine How Unhappy We Will Be

One freezing winter night, my friend Joseph Telushkin got a flat tire while driving to deliver a speech. With not enough time available to call for a tow truck, Joseph endured the cold as he tried to change the tire on his own. But it was to no avail.

Joseph missed an important speech, disappointed an audience, lost money, and had a miserable evening. But as I found out when we spoke the next day, he wasn't particularly unhappy about all this.

"I am convinced that each of us has a flat-tire quota," he told me. "And I had never had a flat tire before."

Many people would have been considerably more unhappy than Joseph in such circumstances. Why wasn't he more unhappy? Because Joseph had a philosophy of life that provided him with a perspective.

We determine how much we will allow something to make us

unhappy. That we can determine our emotional response to events is hard for many people to acknowledge. Most people think that events make them unhappy, that their happiness level is essentially dictated by what happens to them. But this is untrue.

Imagine, for example, two people who lose wallets that contain their credit cards, driver's licenses, money, and important receipts. One of these people is terribly upset for a week. The other is upset for a day. Assuming that the lost wallet was equally important to each person, why did one experience so much more unhappiness than the other? Because he allowed himself to. And a major reason he allowed himself to be unhappy was a lack of perspective on what had happened.

In all my studies of happiness, one of the most significant conclusions I have drawn is that *there is little correlation between the circumstances of people's lives and how happy they are*. A moment's reflection should make this obvious to anyone. We know people who have a relatively easy life and who are essentially unhappy, and we know people who have suffered a great deal but maintained a relatively high level of happiness.

One reason for this is the emotional and psychological disposition with which people are born or that they develop early in life. But innate disposition is not the only explanation for their differing reactions to life. At least as often it is a person's attitude and philosophy of life that determine his or her level of happiness.

The Need for a Philosophy of Life

If innate disposition were the only explanation for why some people are happy despite great adversity and others are unhappy despite myriad blessings, then psychotherapy, religion, and a philosophy of life, not to mention books such as this, would all be useless. Our happiness would be determined by a simple equation: Innate Disposition = Happiness or Unhappiness. In terms of happiness, we would be no more than sophisticated computers programmed to react to events in a given way.

115

But we are not programmed computers. We can determine how we react to events; and we make this determination on the basis of more than disposition. Our reaction is determined by our attitudes and perspective, or more precisely by our philosophy of life, what is known in German as our *Weltanschauung* (worldview).

Without a philosophy of life, we do not know how to react to what life deals us. Our happiness bounces up and down, determined by the day's events and the immediate emotions they elicit rather than by sober reflection. Without being able to place events into perspective—which comes from having a philosophy of life—we are at the mercy of events. Our ship has no destination and no compass.

I have seen this repeatedly. A man in his forties who had just lost his beloved and only brother, his best friend, to a sudden heart attack confided in me that he had completely lost faith in God. Although he was never involved in an organized religion, he told me that he had talked to God every day of his life. But now that his brother had died at such an early age, this man was through with God.

I asked him whether he had ever wrestled with the problem of reconciling unfair death with God's existence before his brother died. After all, many men and women other than his brother have died young and left grief-stricken loved ones behind. How had he understood God in light of *their* losses?

He admitted that he had never really thought about the problem. Those were others' losses, and he somehow felt that given his daily close rapport with God, such a thing wouldn't happen to him.

Now, ten years later, true to his word, he has still not said another word to God.

I know this man to be particularly intelligent and altruistic, so the problem here was not one of self-centeredness or foolishness. This man's problem was that he had never thought through the issue of God and unjust suffering (what is known as theodicy) and had therefore never developed a philosophy of life that could prepare him for such an event. Had he done so, his relationship with God would not have died along with his brother.

Most people wait until tragedy strikes before thinking about how to incorporate tragedy into their life. And then the shock is often too great to absorb into their emotional and psychological system. Although it may not always work, a philosophy of life ought to be regarded as an inoculation against despair. Many people have confronted terrible tragedy, retained their faith, and avoided despair—and they have done so thanks in large measure to having a philosophy of life.

It was in speaking to couples who had suffered the most painful loss in life, the death of a child, that I became most aware of the indispensability of a philosophy of life. After learning that most couples divorce after the death of a child, I raised this issue on my radio show. I asked couples who had stayed together after losing a child to tell me what had enabled them to do so. Although there are always psychological and emotional factors unique to individuals, one conclusion seemed to apply to nearly all couples who remained intact and were even capable of striving for some happiness. Before their tragedy—and in some cases even afterward—they had developed a philosophy of life into which they could fit their tragedy.

Perspective derived from a philosophy of life is not only necessary to deal with tragedies; it applies equally to daily travails. My friend Joseph was able to prevent his ruined evening from making him unhappy because he had a philosophy that enabled him to put it into perspective. He believes that we all have "a flat-tire quota," that in the course of a lifetime all of us will experience missed opportunities, flat tires, canceled flights, misplaced valuables, accidents, lost wallets, broken limbs, and much more that is painful though not quite tragic.

Other Providers of Perspective

Joseph's flat-tire quota is but one example of a philosophy that enables us to have perspective and thereby cope with difficulties. Here are seven other examples of widely held philosophies that enable people to get through hard times:

"This Too Shall Pass"

The story is told that the wise King Solomon commissioned a jeweler to fashion for him a magic ring that would cheer him when he was down and sober him when he got too happy. The jeweler came up with such a ring: engraved on it were three Hebrew words, *gam zu ya'avor*, "This too shall pass."

Knowing that most storms pass is an attitude that enables many people to cope with life's difficulties. In fact, everyone should adopt this attitude. Couples, for example, must come to recognize that they will go through difficult times and that if they keep communicating and do not do or say things that are particularly foolish or destructive, these times will pass, and the couple will come out of them healthier and stronger.

Likewise, parents should know that most parents have difficult periods with their children and that most of these crises pass. For example, many parents of teenagers ought to reassure themselves on an almost daily basis that the teenage years actually end and that they and their child will probably survive them intact. Perhaps they ought to adopt an explanation for the teenage years that was once offered to me by a parent who attended one of my lectures.

After my lecture, this man came over to me and told me that he had figured out precisely what happens to young people when they become teenagers. When a child turns thirteen, he explained, extraterrestrials come and remove the young person's brain and replace it with an extraterrestrial brain. Then, sometime after the child's eighteenth birthday, the extraterrestrials return and put back the original brain. This explanation is an example of applying the attitude "This too shall pass."

"That Which Doesn't Kill Me Makes Me Stronger"

The German philosopher Friedrich Nietzsche (not my favorite thinker, but even people we don't like can come up with wise thoughts) said, "That which doesn't kill me makes me stronger."

Of course, this is not always true. Some things that happen to people are so horrible that they are rendered weaker, not stronger. Such horrors are relatively rare, however, and most people are rendered stronger by facing and surviving adversity. Knowing this does not undo any given trauma, but it does mean that something positive—strength and growth—can come from otherwise negative developments.

There Is a Positive Aspect to What Happened

Related to the above is a philosophy of life that holds that something positive can be found or created in almost every negative development. This is central to my own view of life and is vital to happiness. (The next chapter is entirely devoted to this outlook.)

"To Live Is to Suffer"

I return to what Russian novelist Fyodor Dostoyevsky wrote, "To live is to suffer." This was certainly true in Dostoyevsky's nineteenth-century Russia (and even truer in twentieth-century Russia), and it has been true throughout history for much of humanity. While it has not been literally true for my life and for the lives of hundreds of millions of others, especially in the modern developed world, there is wisdom and utility in this view.

Those who hold this view obviously have a viable philosophy of life into which to place their suffering. If you truly believe that to live is to suffer, suffering is normal, not a debilitating shock.

God Allows Unjust Suffering

For those who wrestle with the problem of theodicy, there is no final answer, but there are workable philosophies of life.

One is that God allows nature to take its course, meaning that God allows cancer cells to metastasize in good people just as readily as in evil ones. If it were otherwise, there would be no point to being good—everyone would be good to avoid getting sick.

Another is that God allows evil people to hurt good ones because God gave human beings freedom of moral choice, without which we would be automatons, not human beings.

A third is that God wills whatever happens to us and that although we may suffer and not understand why we are suffering, God has a reason for willing it. This is not my own theology, but it certainly gives many people a viable way to deal with suffering.

A fourth way of reconciling God with unjust suffering is to posit that God does not will any suffering, but that God is there when we call out for comfort, for strength, and for the peace of knowing that there is a caring God and all is not chaos.

Given the Ubiquity of Suffering, I Am Blessed

I have traveled through more than seventy countries, and the suffering I have seen has made a deep impact on me. To see the suffering that afflicts much of humanity and to be aware of recent horrors like the Holocaust, Communist gulags, and the massive butchery in Rwanda, Cambodia, and Algeria make it difficult to allow oneself to become unhappy over far lesser problems.

Belief in an Afterlife

While our thoughts and actions should be focused on this life, a philosophy of life that posits something after this life, where ultimate justice somehow unfolds, has enabled more people to cope with suffering than perhaps any other philosophy. Whether there really is an afterlife is, of course, neither provable nor disprovable, and arguments for its existence are beyond the purview of this book. I happen to believe in an afterlife because I find it inconceivable that a just God would make an unjust world and that a nonphysical God would make only a physical world. But even those who do not believe that there is a just and nonphysical God and who therefore do not believe in a just afterlife must acknowledge that those who do believe in one are more likely to have a viable philosophy that incorporates unjust suffering and more likely to be happy. To believe that this life is all there is and that those who unfairly endure terrible suffering have nothing to look forward to is not a recipe for happiness.

In sum, a philosophy of life gives our life meaning by enabling us to make sense of it and enabling us to determine how unhappy the negatives in our life will make us. Thus a philosophy of life, more than our innate disposition, is what determines how happy or unhappy we will be. No matter how old you are, it is never too late to develop a philosophy of life. But parents can bequeath their children a priceless gift by offering them a philosophy of life. It will do more to ensure a child's future happiness than almost anything else a parent can give.

Chapter 23

Find the Positive

Example One:
The Ground-Floor Apartment

When I was looking for an apartment in Manhattan as a graduate student at Columbia University, the only one available to me was on the ground-floor, and I rented it. When I mentioned this to New Yorkers, they winced. I had made a big mistake, they would all tell me. Ground-floor apartments are to be avoided—they are the most easily burglarized. These reactions, and the fact that the area in which I rented was a high crime area, could easily have made me unhappy over my choice.

They had no such effect on me. Instead of becoming unhappy, I developed a series of reasons to believe that a ground-floor apartment was the best choice: unlike almost everyone else in the apartment building, I would never have to wait for the elevator; I had immediate access to the superintendent, who lived in the next apartment; moving in and out was cheaper and faster; and I never had to worry about climbing flights of stairs when the elevator broke.

As a result, instead of regretting what I had done and worrying about it, I loved that apartment from the day I moved in (moreover, it was never burglarized, and I became somewhat of a big brother to the superintendent's son).

As I have matured, I have cultivated this blessedly innate tendency to find the positive in almost all situations. Some people accuse those of us who have this attitude of deluding ourselves in order to be happy, but these people miss the point. There is almost always a positive element in a negative situation, just as there is almost always a negative aspect to a positive situation. Choosing to find the positive and emphasizing it is not in any way a form of self-delusion.

Example Two:
Boring and Other Bad Dates

To cite another example that served me well: When I was single I faced the problem of boring dates. Singles widely regard this as an insurmountable obstacle, not to mention a sheer waste of time. As one who has always feared losing time more than losing money and who is almost as easily bored as a four-year-old, I was the perfect candidate for having—and loathing—boring dates. Yet I can honestly say that I never felt that even the most boring date was a waste of time.

Thanks to applying my philosophy of finding the positive in every situation, I turned boring dates—especially the most boring dates—into learning experiences: I decided to find out what rendered a person boring. This is meant to be neither sarcastic nor disparaging—being boring is not a character defect (in fact, many people find evil people particularly interesting). It is meant only to provide an example of how to turn a situation that most people find entirely negative into a positive one.

The more boring I found my date, the more questions I would ask her to try to determine the roots and characteristics of being a boring person—and therefore also of being an interesting one. I believe that I learned much about that area, and I later applied these insights in lectures to young people—hoping to help them to become more interesting people. I learned, among other things, that some people lack passion and that a lack of passion makes people uninteresting; that a lack of introspection makes people boring; that being interested only in oneself or only in macro subjects makes a person boring; and I learned how and why *I* get bored. In short, I grew from boring dates. *If you value growth, you will value virtually every situation* because there are very few situations from which you cannot learn and therefore grow.

Then there were the bad dates, dates with women who were not necessarily boring but with whom I had almost nothing in common or, on rare occasions, actually disliked. I learned even more from these dates. I learned, first, about me. Why didn't I have any chemistry with this woman? What rendered me so different from her? What was it that perhaps *I* lacked that prevented me from liking this person more?

We can use bad or boring dates, dinner parties, and meetings to learn about people. In general, we associate socially only with those with whom we have much in common. Boring and bad meetings therefore provide rare opportunities to learn about people with whom we would otherwise never spend ten minutes.

Value Growth, and You Will Value Virtually Every Situation

Of course, ground floor apartments and bad dates are not among life's most difficult situations. But the rule that something positive can be found in virtually every situation holds in nearly all situations.

Before citing other examples, it is crucial to point out that the fact that we can find good in virtually every situation is in no way the same as the belief that "everything turns out for the best." That belief is, unfortunately, nonsense. There are innumerable instances of things not turning out for the best. To deny this is to deny the reality of the horrors that too many people have experienced. Is the dying murder victim supposed to believe that this is turning out "for the best"? Should the victims of Nazism, the gulag, the Khmer Rouge, the Maoist Cultural Revolution, and the Rwandan genocide, to name just a few of the twentieth century's best known horrors, view the atrocities committed against them and their loved ones as "for the best"? If your child is killed by a drunk driver, how is that possibly "for the best"?

Having said this, the fact remains that most of the bad situations we encounter do have some good that we can extract or, if there is no good to extract, turn into good (the proverbial "turning lemons into lemonade"). As described in Chapter 17, my nephew Joshua Prager turned a terrible situation—being paralyzed after being hit by a truck—into a very positive one. Joshua had planned to be a doctor, played the trumpet beautifully, and was a fine athlete. After the accident he had to drop his plans to be a physician and could no longer play the trumpet or participate in any sport. On the other hand, as a result of the accident he forced himself to develop interests and to discover abilities in himself—such as writing—that he might otherwise never have developed or discovered; he has gained insight and wisdom beyond his years; and he has helped numerous victims of paralysis. Now a reporter for the *Wall Street Journal*, he is probably happier than he has ever been. He turned a bad situation into a positive one (without for a moment denying the bad).

If you break your leg and are laid up for a month, see it as a chance to do some serious reading. If you cannot find a spouse, see it as an opportunity to develop deep and lasting friendships and as a chance to devote far more time to work and interests that you love. If you are married, cannot conceive a child, and choose not to adopt a child (often an irrational but common decision),* see it as an opportunity

---

*The decision of people who want a child not to adopt one is irrational for many reasons, and they are explained in my book *Think a Second Time* (in the essay on "Baby Richard," a four-year-old boy taken from his parents by order of the Illinois Supreme Court in 1995 and given to the biological father who had never seen the boy). Suffice

to concentrate on your marriage and to become loving adults to others' children. Children need all the adult love they can get. And adults other than parents often touch children in ways that parents cannot.

Rabbi Harold Kushner lost his son to a prolonged and terrible illness. Instead of only grieving (and grieving over losses is indispensable to happiness), he took this terrible blow and helped millions of others cope with tragedy—through his book *When Bad Things Happen to Good People* and his lectures.

Those who choose to find the positive that can be found in virtually every situation will be blessed. Those who choose to find the awful in every situation will be cursed. As with happiness itself, this is largely your decision to make.

---

it to note here that a decision not to adopt a newborn is rooted much less in reason than in feelings or beliefs—such as that one will not love an adopted child as much as a biological child (entirely false) or that we know the child's gene pool when we have a biological child and are therefore less likely to encounter genetically based emotional and psychological problems (mostly false: we do not know much about our own gene pool, and to the extent that we do, it is often no more promising than a gene pool about which we know little or nothing).

Chapter 24

Accept Tension

We humans do not like pain, and we therefore seek to avoid it. However, as discussed earlier, trying to live free of pain assures an unhappy life.

Tension provides a good example. Since tension is painful, people try to avoid it, and in so doing they decrease their chances for happiness. For tension is necessary to all growth. A life without tension is a shallow life; so shallow that an absence of tension characterizes animal or plant life more than it does human life. If you have tension in your life, it means that you face competing demands—a characteristic of a full life, not an unhappy one.

We think that we want no tension, but after a moment's reflection we realize that it would be terrible to have no tension. For example, do we want no sexual tension? Isn't it better for a couple to experience sexual tension than not? Don't we even want to experience some sexual tension outside of our marriage, such as having sexual reactions to people other than our spouse and not acting upon them? Doesn't this mean that we are alive and vibrant? As my father, Max Prager, likes to say (and my mother agrees), "The day I stop looking, bury me." Do we want no tension in our work? Has anyone ever accomplished anything with no tension?

The more we are involved in life and the richer our life, the more tension we will experience. The only way to avoid tension is to numb oneself (which is the appeal of drug addiction) or to lead such a dull life that there are no competing demands. Maturity and happiness demand dealing with tension, indeed welcoming it. What we do not want is unnecessary tension, or what we usually call stress or aggravation.

Stress or Aggravation

Although both are painful and inevitable, there is a significant difference between necessary tension and unnecessary tension, or what we will call here stress or aggravation. Tension is usually a sign of vibrancy and health and therefore should not create unhappiness, while continuous stress or aggravation is usually unhealthy to both body and happiness and should be reduced as much as possible.

Aggravation or stress kills—as do many other things in life, such as cigarettes. But stress is worse than cigarettes. Cigarettes at least give some pleasure before they cause the premature death of about one out of every three smokers. Aggravation, on the other hand, only provides pain and probably kills more people than cigarettes.

If you are under a great deal of stress, you must identify the source as precisely as possible and do whatever you can to either remove it from your life, learn to live with it, ignore it, or at the very least, minimize it.

How, ultimately, can you distinguish between aggravation and tension? I would offer two criteria. First, are you growing through it? If you are growing, what you are experiencing should be regarded as necessary tension; if you are not growing, only suffering anguish, it is unhealthy aggravation. Second, if you are incapable of being happy because of what you are experiencing, it is aggravation, not healthy tension. For example, having to do a daily three-hour radio show, without guests, creates tension. But this tension helps create a good show, which is ultimately a source of happiness for me. On the other hand, when I have had to fight with management on behalf of show topics that I believed in, it was simply aggravation, and I had to struggle to maintain my level of happiness.

A life filled with tension can be a deeply happy one. A life filled with aggravation or stress cannot.

Chapter 25

Everything Has a Price
—Know What It Is

There Are No Free Lunches

The Nobel laureate economist Milton Friedman was once asked if he could summarize the essence of economics in a sentence.

"There are no free lunches," he responded.

This is as good an understanding of life as it is of economics. *Everything* has a price. With regard to happiness, there are three rules related to this law of life:

1. Make peace with the fact that *everything* in life has a price.

2. Determine what that price is for anything you desire.

3. Choose whether to pay that price or to forgo what you desire.

Unless you follow all three of these rules, happiness is unattainable—because you will constantly be angry at the prices you pay for everything you have and everything you do.

To Marry or Not to Marry

One classic example of how important it is to think through the prices paid concerns the question of whether to marry or stay single. *Each has great advantages, and each demands a great price.*

If you decide to remain single, you will gain obvious advantages—such as more freedom to do what you please when you please, not having to put up with anyone else's bad moods and idiosyncrasies (and not having anyone else to confront *your* bad moods and idiosyncrasies), and freedom to date whomever you want.

On the other hand, if you decide to marry, you will also gain obvious advantages—such as a partner in life, freedom from the dating scene, stability, and the growth that can only come from long-term commitment to another person.

You cannot have all the advantages of each choice. A good marriage can allow for a fair amount of personal freedom, but no matter how free, a marriage cannot approach the personal freedom of being single. Likewise, you can have loving relationships if you are single, but they cannot approach the depth that a good marriage can.

A common problem in marriage, as in so many other areas of life, is that too many people want the advantages of being both married and single at the same time. They refuse to pay the price for being married. These people—usually men—want the security, the love, and the family that are the results of married life *and* the personal and sexual freedom that characterize single life.

It takes maturity to recognize that this is impossible. There is no way to avoid paying some price. Wise people will weigh the advantages of the married and the single state, take their needs, nature, and values into account, and come to a decision; and once they have decided, they will not spend their time regretting whatever prices they have paid.

To use my own life as an illustration, I long loved the freedom of being single (I didn't marry until I was thirty-two). But I always knew that I would marry. First, I wanted children, and I have always believed that it is wrong to have children outside of marriage; children deserve to start out life with a married mother and father. Second, I knew myself well enough to know that if I remained single, I wouldn't grow nearly as much as I would as a married man. I knew that I would live the life, in George Gilder's wonderful description of single men, of a "naked nomad." I would wander from woman to woman, from bed to bed, pursuing a life of sensual excitement.

When I finally married, I did so after thinking through the prices paid for remaining single and for being married. Marrying with such rational thinking about prices paid may strike some people as unromantic, yet a sober awareness of prices paid is far more likely to lead to permanent love than marrying based on romantic feelings alone. In every marriage, there are moments of greater and lesser feelings of being in love, greater and lesser feelings of passion. During the lesser moments, the rational faculties remind you why you chose to marry.

On the other hand, I have two close male friends who have chosen to remain single. They deeply respect the institution of marriage, and they recognize the prices they pay for not being married. But they know themselves, and they have decided that *for them* the prices of marriage are too high.

Most single people look at happily married couples and sometimes wonder if they have made the right choice. Likewise, married people look at singles and sometimes wonder if they made the right choice. This is natural, and married people need to recognize that sometimes wishing they were single is entirely normal and compatible with a good marriage.

Whether you choose to be married or to be single, knowing the prices that must be paid in either case enables you to pay them, as you eventually must, with much more acceptance and far less anger.

To Have Children or Not to Have Children

The decision to have a child is another example of a decision that must be made with as much awareness as possible of the prices to be paid. Going into marriage without considering the prices of being married is far less dangerous than going into parenthood without being aware of the prices that having children exacts. Marriages, after all, can be dissolved, and the people involved can move on. But parenthood cannot be dissolved; children cannot "move on" if a parent abandons them.

It is easy to understand why nature made conceiving children as pleasurable and as easy as possible—nature cares about the perpetuation of the species. But nature cares not one whit about the happiness of a species' individual members. The ease with which children are conceived has been tragic for untold numbers of people. Too many people become parents solely as a result of sexual pleasure, not as a result of deep thought about the responsibilities of parenthood or the prices to be paid for having engaged in that act of sex. As my father has frequently said, "You need a license to sell pretzels, but any jerk can have a child."

There are immense prices paid for having children and immense prices paid for not having children. These prices need to be weighed with greater care than for any other decision in life. Whatever the decision, the prices paid in each case are steep. That is why I have never tried to convince anyone to have children, though I have tried to convince many people (especially men) to get married. For the sake of society and for the sake of individuals, the vast majority of people should get married. But for the sake of society and for the sake of the individuals involved, many people should never be parents.

Prices Paid for Having Children The prices for having children are discussed in the chapter on family. But to briefly restate them here:

- Children bring enormous challenges to any marriage, no matter how good they or the marriage are.

- Children greatly reduce the amount of personal freedom that parents have.

- Children prevent couples from spending nearly the amount of intimate time with each other that they otherwise would.

- Children greatly reduce the time that parents have to pursue any of their own interests.

- Children make you permanently vulnerable. From the moment your child enters your life, you realize how vulnerable you have become. Their pains are greater than your pains. You worry about their happiness, their health, their intelligence, their success, their friends, whom they will marry, their being hurt, and, of course, about their dying before you do.

- Children cost a great deal of money.

Prices Paid for Not Having Children   On the other hand, the prices paid for not having children are also great—and for me far greater, which is why I chose to become a father. Those who do not have children do not have the following opportunities:

- To bestow love on children. Those who have a great deal of love to give can have no more desirous recipients than children.

- To receive children's love and to come home to a child who runs to you with a hug, among the most powerful emotional experiences available.

- To experience parenthood, an incomparable teacher about life and people.

- To give to one's child what you may not have received from your parent(s) when you were a child. Many men of my generation, for example, grew up at a time when few fathers were emotionally demonstrative to their children. Expressing love to their children is an opportunity for these men to fill an emotional hole.

- To create and experience family life as an adult.

- To have grandchildren.

- To pass on one's religion and values to another generation (though this can be done without having one's own children).

Without children, you pay the price of not having any of this. When things get difficult with any of my children, I can remind myself that I willingly chose to be a father knowing that steep prices would be paid. When you feel that you knew the price in advance and chose to pay it, you are in a far better position to accept life's problems.

The Rule Applies to Everything

The importance of the rule that everything comes with a price probably cannot be overstated. It is therefore very unfortunate that most people do not regularly apply it. Let us make this clear: this rule applies to *every action* people undertake. If you ever think that there is no price being paid for a decision you have made, *you have not thought the issue through.*

Some people may perceive having always to ask, "What price do I pay?" as depressing. It is not at all depressing; in fact, it immeasurably adds to your happiness. First, it enormously helps to prevent unhappiness caused by later shock and disappointment when you do become aware of the prices paid. Second, this rule makes it clear that *whatever else you would choose would also exact a price,* very possibly a much steeper one.

Knowing that you must pay a price for everything you *do*—or choose not to do—is no more depressing than knowing that you must pay a price for everything you *buy.* The more often you ask, "What is the price?" the better equipped you will be to handle life's problems.

Since this rule applies to everything you do, a good idea is to practice it for a few days even with seemingly trivial matters. Here is a silly but real example: If I floss my teeth regularly, I pay the price of spending time doing something I really don't enjoy doing and of not being able to get my tired body into bed as quickly as I want. On the other hand, if I don't regularly floss, I may one day suffer from gum disease and tooth decay. Which price do I prefer to pay?

135

Here is another: If I watch a couple of hours of television tonight, I will enjoy it and find it relaxing. On the other hand, I will probably forget everything I saw by tomorrow morning and may well feel that it wasn't worth hours of my time. Moreover, I will not have spent that time interacting with a child, spouse, friend, or other live human, reading a good article or book, or writing anything.

When choosing a line of work, the question of prices is essential, yet many people do not pose it. Instead they choose to see only the positive in the profession they chose, often only the financial and glamorous benefits. For example, in America at this time, pursuing a career in law is particularly popular (at current rates of law school enrollment, by 2076, I am told, every American will be a lawyer). Yet based on the number of people who later quit practicing law, it would seem that many people who choose to become lawyers do not confront the most important questions anyone should ask about work: Will I enjoy it? Will it add meaning to my life? (Enjoying work and finding it meaningful are the ways work increases happiness—see Chapter 10, on equating happiness with success.)

Whatever line of work you choose exacts a price. The number of hours you work exacts a price. The number of children you have exacts a price. There is a price paid in owning a house, as there is to living in an apartment, or living in the city, or living in the country. There are prices paid for leading a religious life, and there are prices paid for leading a secular life. There are prices paid for living near your parents and prices paid for moving to another city.

The list of prices paid is as long as the list of activities in which we engage, because each one exacts a price. Here, as everywhere else in life, therefore, happiness demands clarity (determining what the prices are) and maturity (deciding what to do and then not complaining—at least, not too much).

Chapter 26

Accept the Lower Parts
of Your Nature

Our Lower Parts Make Us Human—
and Potentially Great

Everyone has miserable parts. We have tendencies toward meanness, selfishness, envy, cruelty, gluttony, dishonesty, lust, avarice, irre-
sponsibility, and hedonism. A few of us have all these tendencies, and
all of us have some of these tendencies. In fact, the very best people
have tendencies toward all or nearly all of these negative traits—
because great character is defined by our struggle with the worst
parts of our nature rather than by not having these parts.

The most important thing to understand when it comes to our
baser parts is not only how normal and natural it is to have them but
that *there is nothing wrong* in having them. Bad is *doing* bad, not *thinking*
bad (there are exceptions—see the next chapter), and it is certainly not
merely having bad *tendencies*.

When I entered adolescence, I was often bewildered by the rotten parts of my nature. With all my religious and moral training, I didn't know what to make of my darker parts. I wondered how a gentle soul like me(!) could have such tendencies. It took me awhile to incorporate my religion's central teaching that deeds, not thoughts, determine a person's decency. Once I did, I made peace with these darker parts, eventually learned why I had them, and learned how to control them.

The only people who have no bad tendencies are dead—either literally or figuratively. To be fully alive, indeed to be fully human, is to have dark tendencies. These are among the aspects of our nature that make us most human and give us our character and passions.

The lower and bad parts of human nature are not only unobjectionable, they can actually be beneficial. Think about it: would you rather be married to a faithful person who has little lust or to a faithful person who has a lustful nature that he or she controls? Most of us would prefer the latter—because that person is both more alive and more moral (there is no virtue in not acting on a desire that doesn't exist).

This is why people with passionate, even wild natures are usually far more interesting—and desirable—especially to the opposite sex. Unfortunately, however, many people often mistakenly assume that people who control their lower passions do not have them. Many women, for example, find themselves repeatedly attracted to men who do not control their passions—and are repeatedly hurt by them— while they reject equally passionate men who do control themselves, erroneously dismissing these men as less exciting. (This phenomenon is known as "the jerks always get the girl.")

As a religious person, I am saddened when religious people teach that having base thoughts and desires is a sin, sometimes even as sinful as acting upon those thoughts or desires. While a pure mind may be a saintly ideal, for the rest of us mortals controlling our behavior is an enormous enough achievement.

One of the most poignant calls I ever received on my radio show came from a middle-aged man who told me that for ten years he had been the sole financial and emotional support of his sick mother. He loved his mother greatly, he said, but because the burden on him was so great, he sometimes wished that she would succumb to her illness and die. He told me that he was wracked with guilt and considered himself to be an awful son.

I told him that not only was he not an awful son, he was a particularly wonderful one. His thoughts were normal and understandable, and his behavior was exemplary. He was far closer to being a model son than a bad one.

None of us do all the good things we do without some ambivalence. Parents certainly know this. Do parents get up in the middle of the night to calm a crying baby without feeling any annoyance toward that child? What about all the time and money some parents spend on their children's education while depriving themselves of deeply needed vacations—is it wrong for them ever to feel burdened by the child? Rather than feeling guilty about such feelings, such parents ought to be proud of themselves for not acting on them.

Two Extremes: Always Suppressing and Always Expressing

With regard to their baser impulses, I have found that many people adopt one of two extremes: they either constantly suppress these feelings or they constantly act on them.

Because people who want to be good often believe that their lower feelings are sinful, they fear that making peace with them will lead to acting on them. In this view it is best to suppress such feelings. On the other hand, particularly in our time, the opposite tendency has asserted itself. Not only do many people not suppress their negative feelings, they feel that it is self-destructive not to express them verbally and often even behaviorally.

As regards verbal expression, this is generally a healthy development (as long as the words are addressed to the proper people). A mother should be able to tell her husband or a close friend that she is going crazy getting up four times every night to comfort her colicky baby. The man who called my radio show should be able to express to someone his occasional wish that his mother succumb to her illness. But verbal expressions of this kind come with an essential caveat: the mother shouldn't express her feelings to the helpless infant, and the man should not tell his feelings to his mother.

On the other hand, *behavioral* expressions of such feelings are almost never acceptable. Neither of these individuals should *act* on their feelings. If the mother does act them out, she might engage in child abuse (virtually every parent comes to understand how child abuse can happen). If the man who called me acted out his bad feelings, he could end up committing murder. In fact, the contemporary movement in the Western world toward legalizing "doctor-assisted suicide" is in part the acting out of adult children's wishes that elderly parents who are gravely ill die.

We often think that the moral life and the psychologically healthy life are in conflict because the former demands suppression and the latter, expression. This is not true. Not only can one be both moral and psychologically healthy but, at their best, moral behavior and psychological health are complementary. In general, psychological health better enables a person to act morally (though it does not ensure it); and we are most psychologically healthy when we are most capable of controlling ourselves.

A major part of leading a moral life is being able to identify our darker parts and being able to control them, and a major part of psychological health and happiness is learning how to identify these parts and how to defang them. Then we can learn how to express these parts of ourselves innocuously, the subject of the next chapter.

Chapter 27

Allow
Innocuous Expression
of Your Lower Parts

As long as we have negative and dark impulses and feelings but do not act on them, those feelings should not impede either a happy or a good life. This needs to be explained further.

Lower Thoughts versus Evil Thoughts

A distinction needs to be made between *lower* and *evil* with regard to both thoughts and behavior. When I write on religion, I make the distinction in more precise terms—between the *immoral* (i.e., that which is evil) and the *unholy* (i.e., that which is lower but not necessarily evil). The immoral and the unholy are therefore not necessarily the same, even though many religious people think they are. All immoral acts (i.e., acts in which we deliberately hurt an innocent) are also unholy, but not all unholy acts are immoral.

An unholy act violates codes of holiness, not necessarily moral codes. For example, a man looking at pornographic pictures may be engaging in an unholy act, but it is not an immoral act unless he has reason to believe that the models posing were tricked or coerced into doing so; or looking at these pictures detracts from his love for his wife; or, in the most evil instance, the pictures are of children. To cite a less emotionally charged example, a person who eats with his face stuffed into a bowl of food is not engaging in an immoral act, but he is eating in an unholy manner.

To better understand the difference between lower thoughts and evil thoughts, let us return to the man who told me that he sometimes wishes that his long ailing mother would die. These thoughts are obviously neither noble nor holy. But they are not evil either. They could be characterized as evil if they were about him killing his mother. But he never thought about that; he fantasized about her dying of her disease. While that isn't noble, it also isn't evil—it is simply lower.

Lower Thoughts and Feelings

In terms of happiness, lower (as opposed to evil) thoughts are not generally a problem. To abolish all lower thoughts, you would have to become more than a good person; you would have to stop being a person and become an angel. Only angels have no ignoble desires.

Some deeply religious people aspire to abolishing lower thoughts, and they therefore try to avoid contact with much of this impure world. They retreat (a religious term in itself) from the world into monasteries, houses of learning, religious communities, and the like. This desire to root out lower thoughts is the basis of religious preoccupation with sexual matters. It accounts for the Muslims who believe women's bodies should be entirely covered (no sight of female flesh, no lower thought), the Christians who declare masturbation a grievous sin (masturbation being the embodiment of lower feelings), and the Jews who refrain from even so much as shaking the hand of any person of the opposite sex except their spouse (no physical contact, no lower feeling).

At the other extreme, much of the modern secular world has no concept of the holy and therefore has little problem with lower feelings. Thus, for example, sexually explicit billboards and television shows permeate society, a great deal is done to arouse sexual feelings, and foul language in public is common.

Neither extreme is conducive to happiness, because *both extremes produce people preoccupied with lower feelings, not freed from them.* Those who put no reins on their thoughts soon find themselves dominated by the sensual stimuli of modern society. At the same time, those who spend their lives trying never to think about the unholy may hide from much of life and suppress their thoughts and feelings or become like the person who tries not to think about an elephant—that is precisely what they think about most.

The key to happiness here, as everywhere else, is balance. This balance is achieved by acknowledging our animal (lower) as well as our divine nature. When God declares in Genesis, "Let us make man in our image," the *us* may be understood to be God and the animals. We humans are created in the image of God and in the image of animals, and it is wrong to try to eradicate either image. There is a place for our animal nature, and there is a place for our divine nature. Among the least happy people I have encountered are those who do not find a place for both. Religious individuals who try to suppress all their lower thoughts often seem unreal and mechanical, and secular individuals who constantly give in to their lower nature become lost souls, addicted to the pursuit of pleasure.

To be happy, we need to fill our souls *and* to make peace with—though not appease—our animal parts.

Evil Thoughts and Feelings

While *lower* thoughts are part of life and need to be accepted for a happy life, *evil* thoughts are almost always injurious to happiness and should be avoided as much as possible. To explain this, let us return yet again to the man who sometimes wishes his mother would succumb to her illness. As noted above, he does not think about killing her. But if he did, he would most definitely be a less happy person.

His happiness would suffer because of his guilt over thinking about murdering his mother and because dwelling on violent, evil thoughts makes a person unhappy. All of us are aware of the different effects that kind and evil thoughts have on our emotional state.*

Acting on Evil Thoughts

If evil *thoughts* help to destroy happiness, then how much more so does evil *behavior*. (If doing evil made people happier, the human species would self-destruct. But the problem is not that doing evil increases happiness; indeed, it decreases it. The problem is that doing evil increases *immediate pleasure*.)

Evil behavior is behavior that hurts an innocent person, and it is always to be avoided, for the sake of both a moral and a happy life. Thus no matter how much a man may wish that his long-ailing mother would die, he must not *do* anything that would hasten her death. That would be evil. He must make peace with his feelings; but he must not act upon them. Similarly, a woman may wish that her husband's ex-wife (or ex-husband's current wife) would die; but she cannot harm the woman.

If people understood the connection between evil and unhappiness, there would be considerably more good—and more happiness—in our world.

---

*All evil thoughts are self-destructive, but not all *violent* thoughts are either evil or self-destructive. There is a difference between evil and violence. Not every act of violence is evil (e.g., police use of violence to subdue violent criminals). Thus while all evil thoughts are destructive, not all *violent* thoughts are. European Jews who fantasized about killing Nazis during the Holocaust in World War II were engaging in a healthy desire to free themselves from the clutches of a death machine. On the other hand, Jews who after the war frequently thought about killing Germans were making themselves miserable (and since not all Germans were Nazis, were also having evil thoughts).

Acting on Lower Feelings: Vice in Moderation

What do we do with our lower parts?

On the one hand, the human being can be likened to a pressure cooker: if the pressure that life inevitably produces is never allowed some release, we will explode either inside (depression) or outside (violence). On the other hand, if we always give in to our lower feelings, we will lead miserable lives, not grow, and end up lonely because few people love the self-absorbed.

I therefore offer an argument for enabling these lower parts to have some expression, or to put it another way, to permit ourselves to engage in moderate vice. A little alcohol, a little tobacco, a little overspending, a little gambling, a little sexually explicit material, a little too much television—these are not ennobling pursuits, but for most people they can offer a helpful release. The problem with all of these is that they can easily become addictive—and then they are vehicles to misery. Many people therefore cannot engage in some or any of these things even in moderation. If you are one of those people, identify those activities to which you can become addicted, and *never* engage in them. Like an alcoholic, you should not believe you can do a little.

Most people, however, can moderately engage in some or all of these activities. Many people can occasionally go to a casino, set a reasonable limit on the money they are prepared to lose, enjoy some gambling, and stop when they have lost the predetermined amount. Some people cannot. They should never set foot in a casino.

Many people can control their use of alcohol. They will drink socially or enjoy a nightly martini without any addictive effect. Others cannot and should never even have a beer.

Moderation has a bad name because it sounds boring. The truth is, however, that if you are moderate in your habits but passionate about life, you are more likely to enjoy more of life than if you either always give in to your lower urges or never do.

Learning about our lower parts and how to express them innocuously is vital to our happiness.

145

Chapter 28

Seek to Do Good

Too many people believe that if there is any relationship between goodness and happiness, it is an inverse one—that to paraphrase the immortal words attributed to baseball manager Leo Durocher, "Good guys finish last." It is easy to understand why people believe that doing good and being happy are unrelated or even contradictory. We look around and see people cheating, getting away with it, and then benefiting from it. Long before Leo Durocher, people grappled with the question "Why do good people suffer and evil people prosper?"

There is no doubt that doing something immoral often brings immediate benefits. *If doing the bad thing never brought benefits, no one would ever do it.* People cheat precisely because there can be immediate benefits to cheating. People lie, steal, murder, and rape for the same reason.

The meaningful question concerning the relationship between goodness and happiness relates to the long run: over the course of a lifetime, are good people more likely to be happier than bad ones? I believe the answer is yes for two reasons. One reason is inner peace. Think of all the truly decent people you know personally, and then think of the worst people you know. Which individuals strike you as having more inner peace? Whenever I have posed this question to audiences, the response has been virtually unanimous. We regard the good people we know as having much greater inner peace.

I have found this to be true both in my personal life and through my research—which leads us to the second reason that goodness brings people greater happiness. If you go through life cheating others, you will go through life expecting others to cheat you. Liars expect to be lied to; cheaters expect to be cheated; and so on. This is why one of the worst human beings of the twentieth century—a century in which there was a great deal of competition for that title—the Soviet tyrant Josef Stalin, was paranoid. He went through life expecting others to treat him as he treated others.

This in turn leads to another unhappy consequence of leading a bad life—loneliness and a lack of love. The bad may have money, power, and fame, but they do not have friends (though they may well have sycophants). According to Albert Speer, Adolf Hitler's one confidant, Hitler had no friends and showed human emotion only when relating to his pet bird. Did Hitler therefore suffer in any way commensurate to the unspeakable suffering he brought to tens of millions of innocent people? Of course not. That would be impossible. He would have to be tortured all day, every day for the next century to begin to feel the suffering that he caused.

I do not argue, therefore, that bad people experience in this lifetime the suffering that they deserve. I only argue that the bad are less happy and have less inner peace, less love, and fewer, if any, friends than good people. And being surrounded by finer people, receiving more love, and having friends are significant contributions to happiness.

Goodness and Happiness Are Predicated on the Same Quality

Perhaps the greatest theoretical argument for the link between goodness and happiness is that the most important characteristic for both of them is the same—gratitude. One cannot be a good person without gratitude, and one cannot be a happy person without gratitude. This provides a vital link between goodness and happiness.

Consequently, even if you are more interested in being happy than in being good, you will still have to cultivate the most important ingredient to both qualities. By becoming more grateful in order to be happy, you will also become a better person because gratitude will make you better. This is one reason why I believe we are designed to be good even though human nature is not basically good (human nature is neither good nor evil; we have tendencies in both directions—see my discussion of human nature in *Think a Second Time*).

In sum, most people can verify from their own experience that people become happier and attain more inner peace as they become better people. Just compare your feelings of happiness after engaging in a particularly good act with your feelings after engaging in any bad acts you have performed. This is the "secret" of every great religion and philosophical system—the more you reach outside of yourself and your ego and do good, the more peace you will attain.

The problem is that one needs to be wise to understand this, and few people are wise until late in life. Ask older people if they have any regrets about their lives. It is unlikely that they will have regrets about any of the good they did; if they have regrets, they are likely to be over the wrong things they did.

Chapter 29

Develop Self-Control

It should be obvious that if human nature is the single greatest obstacle to happiness, controlling our nature is the single greatest step toward happiness. Yet when people think or write about happiness, self-control is rarely stressed.

There are several reasons for this. First, self-control is difficult, and most people want easy paths to happiness.

Second, self-control sounds like a "downer." When most people think about happiness, they think about having fun and getting what they want. Self-control connotes the opposite of these things; it implies denying yourself fun and other things you want. Saying no to yourself does not sound like the royal road to happiness.

Third, self-control doesn't sell. Imagine two books featured in a bookstore: One is titled *Happiness—Keep Saying Yes to Yourself!* The other is titled *Happiness—Keep Saying No to Yourself!* Which is more likely to sell?

Fourth, self-control goes against the *Zeitgeist,* the spirit of our times, which glorifies getting all we want and makes us feel deprived and even somewhat of a failure if we do not. If medieval religious attitudes are associated with self-denial, modern secular attitudes are identified with denying ourselves nothing.

Yet happiness is *impossible* without self-control. In fact, everything we want is impossible without self-control. Ask anyone who has achieved what you particularly desire to achieve, and you will find a profoundly self-disciplined individual. The *Wall Street Journal* published an article about American millionaires who were not born into wealth and found that the most common characteristic among them was self-control.

If you want financial success, you need the self-control to waste little time on fun things that don't contribute to your personal and professional development. If you want happy and healthy children, you need the self-control to spend a great deal of time with them (thus depriving yourself of time to do what you want to do for yourself). If you want to be physically fit, you need the self-control to eat less fattening, less delicious foods and to exercise regularly.

Self-control gives you something else that is crucial to happiness—freedom. Unfortunately, however, many people define the great value of freedom incorrectly. They define freedom as doing whatever they want. But doing what you want usually means doing what your body and nature want, and this is not only not freedom, it is actually more akin to bondage. Addicts do what they want—and they are among the least free people on earth. *Freedom is being able to do what will bring you happiness*—and that takes constant self-control.

How to Develop Self-Control

I offer two guidelines for developing self-control.

The first is to develop habits of self-control. We are so much creatures of habit that it almost doesn't matter whether those habits are constructive or destructive. If you habituate yourself to exercise self-control, you will find it difficult to stop, and if you habituate yourself to lazy habits, you will find it equally difficult to stop.

The second guideline is to never lose sight of your goal. If you never lose sight of your goal, you will always know what you have to do to achieve it and therefore be less likely to give in to your nature and do what it wants rather than what your goal demands. By keeping the prize—your goal—clearly in mind, it will be easier to exercise the self-control necessary to achieve it. It is very difficult to exercise self-control if there is no prize in sight.

Ideally you will adhere to both guidelines all the time.

For example, let us say that you want to write a book. Constantly keep the prize—the happiness you will derive from having written a book—in mind. Then you are more likely to exercise the self-control you need to make a habit of sitting down regularly to write your manuscript.

If you want to raise good children, constantly keep the prize—happy, productive future adults—in mind, and develop certain habits that enable you to realize that goal. For example, in raising my children, I have followed the rule that no matter what I am doing (including writing a book), I will always respond to my children's request for attention. I made this a rule because I knew that if I didn't, I would always find a good reason not to pay attention to my children. Since I am always doing something that I think is important, I knew that waiting for some moment when I was not doing something important really meant *never* getting up when my children called. I kept my mind clearly fixed on the goal—raising emotionally healthy children who knew I loved them—and adopted a rule of behavior that necessitated self-control. I have surely made my share of errors as a parent, but not responding when my children called is not one of them.

Keeping your mind on the goal you most desire in order to maintain the self-control necessary to achieve the goal is another example of our mind, not our immediate feelings, dictating our behavior in order to be happy. A well-known man once confided to me that during his youngest child's early years, his wife had felt she had to finish a series of paintings in order to feel fulfilled and enjoy some of the public prestige that her husband enjoyed. She therefore did not spend nearly as much time with this daughter as she had spent with her other children. As a result, there was a clear deterioration in the girl's emotional and intellectual growth at that time. Had this woman relied on her mind rather than her feelings, she would probably have had the self-control to postpone intensive painting for a few years and spend more time with her young daughter. She would have ended up with two beautiful works of art—a well-adjusted child and a beautiful series of paintings.

The primary rules, then, for developing self-control are to have clear goals, know what is necessary to achieve them, and develop the habits necessary to do so. Never lose sight of those goals when confronted with daily temptations to do other immediately gratifying things.

It may well be worth your while to set down in writing what it is you most want in life and how that can be achieved. For example:

I want good and healthy children. Therefore I will do the following . . .

I want to get this academic degree. Therefore I will do the following . . .

I want to play a musical instrument. Therefore I will do the following . . .

I want a good marriage. Therefore I will do the following . . .

I want to be in better physical shape. Therefore I will do the following . . .

When you do not do "the following," know that it is not your mind but your fallible human nature that you are obeying.

The only way to get what you ultimately want is to deny yourself short-term pleasures that interfere with your goal.

Chapter 30

Find and Make Friends

Averting Loneliness

The modern era has conquered many diseases, but it seems that one plague of humanity may actually be getting worse—loneliness.

In the most modern, affluent societies, people seem to be doing less with friends or with members of their extended family. There are many reasons for this. Having more personal freedom and opportunities than ever before, many people are far more mobile than ever before. Adult children are not expected to take care of parents as much as in the past—society has taken on much of that responsibility. Even seeking entertainment, heretofore usually a social act, is increasingly possible without even leaving one's home—by watching television or a movie, sitting at the computer, or listening to music. People do not join as many clubs, sing in as many choirs, or attend as many live performances as before. And in major urban centers, crime keeps many people, especially women and the elderly, from leaving their homes after dark.

All of this means that in the modern world people are more likely to be alone.

There are, of course, great benefits to solitude; and being alone does not necessarily mean being lonely. But the human being is a social creature. We don't merely *want* companionship, we *need* it to survive.

Deep human companionship is normally achieved through family, marriage, and friendship. Ideally, we experience companionship through all three, but the good news is that if you cannot find deep companionship in all three, any one of them can be profoundly fulfilling.

Family

Our first deep companionship is found in family relationships. If we are fortunate, we bond to a parent (if we are even more fortunate, we bond to both parents) and to siblings. We may also have the opportunity to find loving relationships with family outside our immediate one—with an uncle or aunt, grandparents, and cousins.

As deeply loving as any of these bonds may be, however, they generally do not assuage loneliness as effectively as marriage and friendship do, because most family relationships are time-bound. When we become adults, most of us spend much less time with our parents, grandparents, uncles, and aunts than we did as children. Indeed, the nature of the child-parent relationship is such that if it is healthy, we do not spend as much time with our parents when we grow up. Family relationships are limited by time for another reason—as we get older, our older relatives begin to die.

Of course, neither of these reasons applies to siblings, and many people do develop ongoing loving relationships with a sibling. This is not the rule, however. Since Cain killed Abel, brothers and sisters have not been known for the closeness of their relationships—even when they love each other.

If we start out life with loving family relationships, our chances for happiness are incalculably increased. It is almost impossible to overstate the importance of those bonds. But as we get older, other relationships usually provide greater opportunities for intimacy because they are not time-bound, and these are relationships with peers.

Marriage

When it is good, marriage is the most profound form of companionship a human can experience.

First, only marriage combines all three forms of companionship —a spouse is family, best friend, and permanent companion. That is why it is widely held that while the death of a child is the most painful loss, the death of a spouse is the most disorienting one.

Second, unlike all other family relationships and unlike all other friendships, marriage alone combines those elements with sex, a uniquely powerful form of bonding.

Third, unlike other family relationships, which are nearly all unequal (parent-child; older sibling–younger sibling), a good marriage is a relationship of equals.

Fourth, unlike both family and friends, we are with our wife or husband virtually every day. And the concept of "quality time" notwithstanding, quantity of time is a quality, one that has a powerfully bonding effect. Women intuitively know this better than men, which is why it is they who generally demand more time with their spouse.

Because of its unique power to fulfill our deep needs for companionship and because of its uniqueness in combining all the forms of companionship, little in life is as good as a good marriage, and little in life is as bad as a bad marriage. Therefore choosing a spouse is one of the two most important decisions of our life (the other is whether to have a child) and must be made as wisely as possible.

Friends

Friends fill a special niche in life. While we cannot choose family—we are stuck, for better and for worse, with the family we are dealt—we do choose our friends. Friends are the people we choose to accompany us through life; they are our chosen companions on this bittersweet journey.

Having been blessed with close friends since childhood, as an adult I have been taken aback to learn how many people do not have close friends. Most people have friends in the sense of having people with whom to periodically dine, play, and chat, but they do not have close friends.

A close friend is a person whom we love, whom we trust, and in whom we can confide (yes, a family member can be such a friend). When thus defined, it is understandable why friends are so important and why they are not plentiful.

Given how important friendship is and how many people do not have close friends, a happier life necessitates finding and making close friends. Yet few adults make finding friends a priority. This is a mistake, but it can be easily rectified. The moment you realize how important it is to have friends, you can begin trying to make friends.

Finding Friends

If you want to bring a friend into your life, you need to go about finding one in much the same way that you go about trying to find a spouse. Once we decide that we want to get married, we begin searching for a mate; we go to social events that maximize our opportunities to meet a kindred spirit, and we begin dating. We should do the same things to find friends, except that the sex of the friend usually ought to be the same as our own (see below).

Most people do not do this. They either attach much less importance to finding friends than to finding a spouse, or they feel that finding friends "just happens," so that no specific efforts are necessary. Both attitudes are wrong.

First, for most people friends are crucial to happiness. (I say "for most people" because I have known a small number of people, mostly of my parents' generation, who claim to have all the friendship they need through their spouse.) Second, friendships no more "just happen" than marriages do. They usually have to be sought and developed.

First, Know Their Values   One way to find friends is to become active in groups whose members are likely to have a high proportion of individuals who share your values. While shared values aren't sufficient for friendship, friendship is impossible without shared values. In fact, one reason people are hurt by those they had considered friends is that friends are too often chosen without attention to their values.

This was brought home dramatically in a call to my radio talk show. A twenty-one-year-old woman called me to tell about her girlfriend, who had been raped and murdered by a man whom the caller had considered a friend. I asked this woman, who had suffered the additional trauma of being the person who discovered her friend's body, whether in retrospect she was shocked by the man's conduct. So shocked, she answered, that she was no longer going out with men. If a man she trusted could do such a thing, how could she ever know what man she could trust?

After assuring her that virtually any man would be as horrified as she was by what that man did, I tried to answer her question. I told her that I have been fortunate in having been shocked very rarely by the behavior of friends. The reason? I know my friends' values. Did she know her murderer-friend's values? I asked.

"What do you mean?" she responded. She didn't know what I was talking about.

I have a simple rule that is of great value in identifying whom to trust: Do not choose friends on the basis of personality, "chemistry," or enjoyment alone. Know their character (i.e., their values and whether they act on these values) before you trust them. My caller trusted someone without having a clue about his values.

Many people do not know their friends' values, and this is a major reason they are often hurt and disappointed by them. If you ignore character and values in choosing your friends, you may be in for great disappointment.

One way to test whether you have chosen your friends wisely is to ask yourself why they are your friends. If your only answer is that you like them and they are fun to be with (certainly important components of friendship), you probably haven't given consideration to their values. Or try this: what case could you make to people who have never met your friends to prove that your friends are good people?

A Guide to Ascertaining People's Values   Since ascertaining character is so important in choosing a friend, how do we go about doing this? How does one determine if a person is a decent person?

There is no foolproof method for identifying character. If there were, intelligence agencies in democracies would never have moles; employers would never be cheated by employees; and police forces would have no rotten apples. But three guidelines should help:

1: You must have good values yourself, and you must be able to identify and articulate those values. It is obviously impossible to ascertain the value system of others if you don't know your own. This is an example of the connection between goodness and happiness. Good people bring good people into their lives, and good people in our lives bring us happiness. The people we bring into our lives are somewhat like a mirror of ourselves—and as with all mirrors, what we see may sometimes disturb us. If you find that you repeatedly bring unsavory people into your life, either there is something missing in your own character or your good character is being sabotaged by a troubled emotional life.

2: Once you are clear about your values, try to ascertain the values of the people you are considering as friends. Talk to them about "heavy" subjects, both personal and general. These topics almost always reveal something about people's concerns, values, and character. You may find out if they have a kind or cold heart, if they live for more than personal success, if they have love in their lives, if they are bigots, and more.

3: Pay as much attention to how these people treat others, especially people from whom they need nothing, as to how they treat you. Watch, for example, how your prospective friends treat waiters and waitresses. Do they treat them as inferiors to be ordered around or with politeness and generosity?

A person's employees or the janitor where the person works can often tell you more about an individual's character than the person's boss or friends can. Waitresses sometimes know a person's character better in ten minutes than do the person's acquaintances of many years. People always treat others decently when they want something from them—for example, friendship, sex, money, marriage. That someone treats you well may therefore reveal nothing about that person's character and therefore give no indication about how that individual will treat you later, under other circumstances.

Why Close Friends Ought to Be of the Same Sex

Thus far we have narrowed our search for friends to people of good character (not angels). I also suggest narrowing the search to people of the same sex. While, of course, it is possible for heterosexuals to have close friends of the opposite sex, it is best to seek friends of the same sex. Close friendships with someone of the opposite sex tend not to last.

One reason is that each of you will probably eventually marry someone else, and the person you marry will become your closest friend of the opposite sex. The intensity of your friendship with your opposite-sex friend will therefore have to be greatly decreased. Your spouse is most unlikely to tolerate your having an ongoing intimate relationship with another person of the opposite sex, even if there is no sexual attraction, let alone sexual relations, between the two of

159

you. It is not sex alone that makes for an intimate relationship, and your spouse has the right to expect to be your one truly intimate friend of the opposite sex.

All forms of intimacy with others can threaten a marriage. Ask a woman how she would feel if her husband had frequent intimate conversations, though no sexual contact, with another woman; and ask a man how he would feel if his wife regularly dined alone with another man, even if the two of them had no sexual contact.

On the other hand, none of these problems need affect same-sex friends because they can easily remain our friends once we are married. Few wives find it troubling that a man retains his close male friends after marrying, and many find it endearing. The same holds true for women retaining their close women friends after marriage.

A second reason to search for friends of the same sex is that with few exceptions, men understand men better than they understand women, and women understand women better than they understand men. Because of this and the absence of sexual tension, most of us feel freer to open up with members of our own sex. And understanding and opening up is what friendship is about. (This is, incidentally, one of the great challenges of marriage—making your husband or wife, even though of the opposite sex, your best friend and the one in whom you most confide.)

A third problem with what are called platonic friendships is that much of the time the friendship is platonic to only one of the friends. Usually in male-female friendships, one of the two friends would like the relationship to be more than platonic. I have repeatedly been told of friendships in which one party was shocked to learn that the other had harbored romantic or sexual desires for them—sometimes for years.

Furthermore, what begins as a platonic friendship between a man and a woman can easily lead to greater desires on the part of one or both. Innumerable marriages started as nonsexual, nonromantic friendships. This is not odd. If a man and a woman confide in each other and love each other—as friends should—it is hardly surprising when erotic attraction develops.

Keeping Friends

Forgive Them Their Flaws Perhaps the most important rule for keeping friends is this: If they are decent people and they have been good friends, *forgive them their flaws*. Every friend you have has flaws because all humans are flawed. Flawless friends (i.e., those who never complain, are always loving, never have moods, are fixated on us, and never disappoint us) are known as pets. Consequently, people who are intolerant of their friends' flaws either remain friendless or end up with animals as their closest friends.

This does not mean that no matter how friends treat you, they must always be forgiven. Nor does it mean that all friendships must be maintained. There are times when friendships must be ended. But ending a close friendship can approximate a divorce in terms of pain and should be done only after careful thought.

When should a hurt mean the end of a friendship? After two judgments are made, taking into account:

- *The friend's record*

    All of us establish a moral bank account in life. Over the course of our lifetime, our acts of decency and integrity are our deposits and our indecent and dishonest acts are our withdrawals. Those with large balances in their accounts deserve the benefit of any doubts we may have about them, and they deserve forgiveness when they have actually made a withdrawal (i.e., done us wrong). Unfortunately, among the many miserable traits of human nature is an unwillingness to assess others' moral accounts accurately. We tend to remember withdrawals (the bad that people do, especially to us) far longer than we remember deposits (the good that people do, even to us). And if we do this to our friends, we will eventually lose all of them.

- *The friend's motive*

    In assessing whether a hurtful act should end a friendship, the other guideline is to determine the motive. Specifically, was it

161

malicious? In general, I believe that when dealing with relationships (of any type), one should try to end the relationship if the person exhibits meanness. There is no reason to tolerate malicious behavior. We don't need enemies if our friends are mean to us. On the other hand, all sorts of nonmalicious behavior must be tolerated if we are to keep any friends—such as hurtful acts motivated by confusion or hurt or anger—but not by meanness or a general lack of decency. In such cases the friendship ought to be preserved. Friends don't grow on trees.*

Don't Burden Friends with Guilt   When friends do things you don't like, even if hurtful (but not mean), don't burden them with guilt. If necessary (and it may not be necessary, because there are parts of everyone that annoy us), say you were hurt, and move on.

A personal example: I love good talk, especially with friends, but I do not like talking on the telephone. Some of my friends love talking on the phone. To their great credit, my telephone-loving friends never instill guilt in me for almost never calling them, and they don't even get angry with me for not immediately returning their phone calls. They know both how much I love them and how much I dislike talking on the telephone. And I assume that they find other qualities of mine that compensate for this one.

Couples Need Couples

When people are single, they instinctively realize how important cultivating friends is. Without friends, a single person is alone virtually all the time. When people marry, on the other hand, they almost instinctively think the opposite—that their need for friendship has

---

*This concern with motives applies only to the motives of intimates. As regards the motives of strangers (i.e., nearly everyone in the world), motives are not particularly important. If I am drowning, I do not care if I am saved by a paid lifeguard who couldn't care less about me personally or by a passerby acting out of altruism or by someone who recognizes and cares for me. Please see my essay, "Don't Judge Motives," in *Think a Second Time*.

been met by marrying. Many couples do not recognize how important it is for couples to have friends.

As already noted, our spouse ought to be our closest friend. But
even when this is the case, a married couple, *as a couple,* can greatly
benefit from having friends, especially other couples. Discussing
marital and family issues with another couple is of great help to a
marriage. Yet few couples do this, which is why people are often surprised when a couple with whom they are friendly separates. Had
these couples talked openly about marital issues, the intact couple
could have, at minimum, been there to comfort the partners during
their troubled time and, at best, actually helped preserve the other
couple's marriage. Most marital discord is not unique to any given
couple but quite universal (because so much of it emanates from
male-female differences). Much marital discord, therefore, could be
reduced by discussing problems with another couple and seeing how
many marital problems the two couples share.

It is difficult to overstate how much stress can be reduced when
people learn that their problems are shared by others. I think of how I
yelled at my young son one day and how intensely embarrassed I was
to realize that my friend, Robert Florczak, was in the next room and
overheard me. God, I wondered, what must he think of me as a
father? Just as I thought this, he walked into the room and said to
me, "You don't know how relieved you just made me feel."

"What do you mean?" I asked.

"I sometimes yell at my son, but I was sure that you *never* yell at
yours. God, am I relieved to know that you do too."

And of course, I was every bit as relieved to find out that he, a
truly gentle soul, sometimes yelled at his young son.

Thank God for friends.

Chapter 31

Psychotherapy
and Religion

Psychotherapy

From the moment of our birth, life cannot give us all that we desire, and often it cannot even give us what we need. Life is difficult even when it is wonderful, and for many people it is only difficult, not wonderful.

Everyone has been wounded. It is almost inevitable that our parents will wound us in some way. If we are not wounded by our parents, we may be wounded by the death or illness of a parent or sibling, by a bitter marriage or bitter divorce, or if our immediate family is close to idyllic, we might be wounded by some other adult who abuses us or peers who mock us. An unscarred childhood is possible but very rare.

As we grow into childhood and adolescence, it is almost inevitable that we will be wounded in other ways. Perhaps it was the death of a friend or relative or an accident that hurt us or a loved one, or we were hurt by our first romantic love or failed in some important competition. As with childhood, few people experience a wound-free adolescence.

For these reasons, you don't have to be abnormal, only human, to benefit from psychotherapy. To deny that psychotherapy can be of help is to deny having any emotional or psychological problems; to deny that any important relationship can be made more healthy, loving, or intimate; or to deny that psychological therapy has merit. To deny having any emotional or psychological problems or that any important relationship can be improved is to engage in self-denial. As for denying that psychotherapy has merit, how, without it, does one treat psychological wounds? If physical wounds necessitate physical therapy, why don't psychological wounds necessitate psychological therapy? It is true that psychotherapy *alone* will never cure all our personal problems, but neither will anything else *alone*—not love, not religion, and not meaningful work, to cite three powerful antidotes to despair. They are all necessary.

Even happily married couples should find the time for marital therapy. Therapy should not be regarded as necessarily fixing what is broken but rather as a device for ensuring that nothing does break. Just as we bring perfectly functioning cars for periodic tune-ups, not because they are broken but so that they do not break, so too marriages need periodic tune-ups to ensure that they remain in good condition.

Psychotherapy's Limitations

As important as psychotherapy is, however, it has three serious limitations as a vehicle to happiness.

Most Therapists Aren't Very Good   Every psychotherapist to whom I have spoken has stated that most therapists are not particularly competent. This is not a slur on psychotherapists, because it is true of nearly all professions. It is merely a recognition of three facts.

First, psychotherapy is an art as much as a science. To be a truly good psychotherapist demands not just knowledge of psychology but wisdom and an innate ability in handling people—two rare qualities in anyone. It may therefore take more talent to be a good psychotherapist than it does to be a good surgeon. A surgeon needs knowledge and great physical dexterity, not a great way with people, wisdom, and common sense.

Second, most people who complete enough courses can become licensed therapists; it takes perseverance more than wisdom, common sense, or even intelligence to become a psychotherapist.

Third, many psychotherapists entered their profession as troubled souls looking for therapy. This can be an advantage when they undergo extensive therapy, are helped by it, and use their insights into themselves in helping patients. But it can be a disadvantage when they do not undergo effective therapy and their own problems cloud their judgment as therapists.

How to choose a psychotherapist is therefore an urgent question—especially since the wrong therapist can actually damage you. I can offer only one general guideline: Be wary of your therapist if you are never challenged and never in pain. A true uncovering of the genesis of your problems must sometimes involve real pain and real self-inquiry. If you are simply made to feel good and/or leave each session convinced that you are fine and all those around you are sick, it may be time to consider looking for a different therapist. You should be spending your hard-earned money to be empowered by honest confrontation with your problems, not merely to hear, "I hear your pain, you poor thing."

Psychotherapy Addresses Only Psychological Obstacles
Psychotherapy alone cannot make us happy, because it addresses only psychological obstacles to happiness. As enormous as those obstacles often are, removing them does not make us happy any more than healing a broken leg makes us track stars. Psychotherapy, if completely successful, removes only psychological obstacles to happiness. This is an enormous achievement, but there are many other obstacles to happiness, as this book demonstrates.

As important as psychotherapy is, many people seek too much from it. It alone cannot make you happy or even undo your problems. Only you, not your therapist and not your therapy, can make you happy—and that involves considerably more than good therapy.

Psychology Has Nothing to Say about Meaning Psychotherapy alone cannot make us happy, because it has nothing to say about the meaning of life—and happiness is impossible without meaning. So important are meaning and purpose to achieving happiness that finding them is even more important to happiness than a healthy psyche. I have met people who are psychologically troubled but who have some measure of happiness—thanks to having a strong belief in the meaningfulness of their life and of life generally. On the other hand, I cannot even imagine a person being happy who lacks purpose and meaning, no matter how much fine psychotherapy he or she has undergone.

This is the major reason many religious individuals persuade themselves that psychology is unimportant and religion is all one needs to be happy. Since religion gives people meaning and purpose and in so doing gives them some happiness, they believe, why bother with psychology? They are wrong.

Religion

Why Religion Isn't Enough

Religion alone is not enough either.

While religion at its best can give a believer more comfort and happiness than even psychology at its best can, religion still cannot give us everything we need to be happy and self-aware. People who are plagued by psychological wounds can certainly find some peace and happiness in religion, but without addressing the psychological roots of their pain they will never be as happy as they can be.

More important, they will be tempted to use religion as a mask to cover the psychological wounds that they refuse to look at. And when religion is used in this way—to mask psychological problems—it can actually make people both psychologically and morally worse than

167

they would have been without religion. When religion is used this way, instead of helping to solve people's psychological problems, it fools them into thinking that they do not have these problems. Consequently, the problems are left to do their damage, while the people walk around thinking they are fine. On the moral plane, the damage can be even greater. Religion can give psychologically impaired people an enormously powerful weapon with which to express their psychological problems and thereby hurt others. Cruel use of religion by psychologically impaired individuals—in family life and in the life of whole societies—is the dark underside of religious history.

There is another, related reason why religion is not enough. A happy person, as opposed to a contented animal, is self-aware. The happiness that the psychologically impaired achieve through religion alone is often the shallow happiness of the unexamined life. This is why some religious people appear simple and unsophisticated—they have retreated from being real (i.e., knowing oneself) to being religious for the great comfort that being religious can provide. This is as unimpressive religiously as it is psychologically. God did not put us here to have the contentment of animals. We are to know as much as we can know—about ourselves and about life—and with that knowledge still be happy.

When we use religion as a shield against knowing ourselves, it is a false use of religion that can only end up distorting it. Religious fanatics are unhappy people who bend religion by and to their troubled psyches. Conversely, the finest of religious people are also the psychologically healthiest—because they are free to find in religion its greatest truths and apply it most healthfully to themselves and to the world.

Why Religion Is Necessary

Though not sufficient, religion is nevertheless necessary for happiness. This will be disputed by some secular readers, who will argue that there are just as many happy agnostics and atheists as there are happy theists.

I doubt it, and some of the most ardent antireligious thinkers in history also doubt it. After all, one of the most potent antireligious arguments has been that religion is, in the well-known words of Marx and Engels, the "opiate of the masses." Even antireligious activists acknowledge the power of religion to provide comfort and happiness. They can argue that religion is a fraud, but they cannot argue that it doesn't bring people happiness.

There is another reason why I doubt that secularists are as likely to be happy as religious people. The more people think, the more they are likely to recognize that if there is no religious meaning to the universe, there is no meaning of any type to the universe. And no thinking person can be truly happy believing that ultimately everything is pointless. In *Annie Hall,* the seven-year-old Woody Allen laments that the universe "is expanding and someday it will break apart, and that would be the end of everything!" He realizes that life is, therefore, pointless. His parents think he is nuts. He isn't.

Aside from giving the universe meaning, religion infuses the individual's day with transcendence, provides a supportive community for life's best and worst moments, teaches gratitude, bonds parents and children, keeps the individual in touch with the past and hopeful for the future, offers the individual regular opportunities to get in touch with the holy, teaches self-control, and provides meaningful holy days, not merely days off—all of which are essential to happiness.

Given the singular importance of knowing the self and experiencing the transcendent, I have long advocated that every clergyman see a psychotherapist and that every psychotherapist go regularly to a house of worship. The clergy of the psyche and the clergy of the soul need each other. And the rest of us need both of them.

Epilogue

Passionate Moderation

Happiness Is a Serious Problem could have been subtitled *The Case for Passionate Moderation*. Throughout the book, one theme that constantly repeats itself is that happiness is attained through moderation.

Many people associate being moderate with being boring, and sometimes it surely is. But for the great majority of people, moderation is essential to happiness, and moderation *includes* passion, excitement, and fun. Indeed, a life without passion, excitement, and fun is not a moderate one; it is an ascetic one.

Every great philosophy, religious and secular, Eastern and Western, has stressed that a happy and good life must emphasize moderation in all things.

I end as I began. The pursuit of happiness is a noble human endeavor, no less so than any other. It is an art that demands no less proficiency than playing a Bach sonata. It is an accomplishment no less worthy than climbing a great mountain. It involves constant use of the mind and constant self-discipline. The route to its attainment confers wisdom and inculcates gratitude. And given its moral ramifications, happiness is no less moral an imperative than, let us say, democracy.

It is no wonder then that for most people, happiness is indeed a serious problem. I hope, dear reader, that my book will have made it less so for you.

Index

DENNIS PRAGER writes and publishes a twice-monthly newsletter, *The Prager Perspective,* and regularly releases tapes of his lectures. For information on his newsletter, tapes, or films, or on how to bring him to lecture before your organization, please write to The Prager Perspective, 10573 Pico Boulevard, Los Angeles, CA 90064. You may also call 800-225-8584 or 310–558–3958 or contact the web site DennisPRAGER.com.